Tales from the Tower

✠

Secrets and Stories from a Gory and Glorious Past

✠

THINK
BOOKS

A THINK BOOK

First published in Great Britain in 2006 by Think Publishing
The Pall Mall Deposit, 124-128 Barlby Road, London W10 6BL
www.think-books.com

Distributed in the UK and Ireland by Macmillan Distribution Ltd.
Houndmills, Brunel Road, Basingstoke RG21 6XS
Distributed in the United States and Canada by Sterling Publishing Co., Inc.
387 Park Avenue South, New York, NY 10016-8810

Published in association with

Historic Royal
PALACES

Author: Fiona Jerome
Editor: Caroline Ball
Think Books: Rica Dearman, Emma Jones, Lou Millward,
Mark Searle, Dominic Scott and Rob Turner
Historic Royal Palaces: Clare Murphy

ISBN-10: 1-84525-026-5
ISBN-13: 978-1-84525-026-3

Printed in Italy by ⬛ Grafica Veneta S.p.A

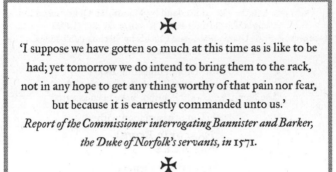

'I suppose we have gotten so much at this time as is like to be had; yet tomorrow we do intend to bring them to the rack, not in any hope to get any thing worthy of that pain nor fear, but because it is earnestly commanded unto us.'

Report of the Commissioner interrogating Bannister and Barker, the Duke of Norfolk's servants, in 1571.

CONTENTS

✠

Plan of the Tower showing the
three wards of the castle and
the principal buildings.

TOWER HILL

Beauchamp
Tower

Pump
House

Middle
Tower

Byward
Tower

Queen's Stairs

N

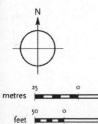

metres

25   0   100

feet

50   0   400

RI

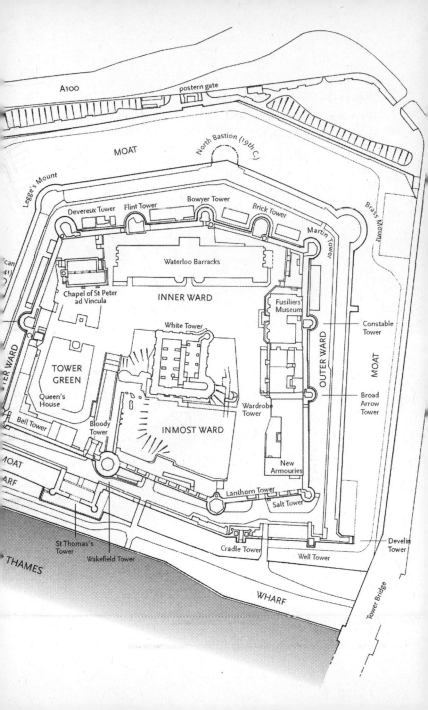

A100

postern gate

MOAT

North Bastion (19th C.)

Legge's Mount

Devereux Tower

Flint Tower

Bowyer Tower

Brick Tower

Martin Tower

Brass Mount

Waterloo Barracks

Chapel of St Peter ad Vincula

INNER WARD

Fusiliers Museum

White Tower

Constable Tower

TOWER GREEN

OUTER WARD

MOAT

Queen's House

INMOST WARD

Wardrobe Tower

Broad Arrow Tower

Bell Tower

Bloody Tower

New Armouries

Lanthorn Tower

Salt Tower

MOAT

St Thomas's Tower

Wakefield Tower

Cradle Tower

Well Tower

Develin Tower

THAMES

WHARF

Tower Bridge

CHAPTER

✠

CASTLE & COUNTRY

✠

In modern London it's hard to appreciate how the Tower of London would once have dominated the skyline. The central keep rose right in the middle of the city's most populous district, towering over even the high walls that surrounded it: a testament to the power of Norman kings. Nowadays, Yeoman Warders in their colourful blue and red tunics take visitors on tours, the clipped-winged ravens peck about the lawns and costumed interpreters re-enact famous scenes from the Tower's history. But 900 years ago, the Tower presented a different picture: it was a symbol of Norman victory over the Saxon English; it was a dominant fortress safeguarding the fledgling city of London.

Setting about subduing the country he had just conquered, William I (1066-1087) began building castles. Within the first year of his rule he had a castle built at the south-east corner of London's old Roman walls, to guard both the city and the river. Baynard's Castle was built near the city walls at Blackfriars, which was located at the westernmost edge of the city, and Mountfichet's Tower was constructed just to the north of that, where Ludgate Circus is today. While these disappeared in early Medieval times, his White Tower endures.

The early castle was enclosed by an earthwork with a wooden palisade on the top. The total area enclosed by the original castle walls is considerably smaller than the 18 acres it covers today. Given what we know of typical Norman castles, which were usually of a motte and bailey design, there may once have been a much larger outer enclosure (or bailey) containing the homes and workplaces of the tradesmen required to keep a castle running, not to mention the garrison.

There are **21** different towers within the precincts
of the **Tower of London**:

Beauchamp • Bell • Bloody • Bowyer • Brick • Broad Arrow
• Byward • Constable • Cradle • Develin • Devereux • Flint
• Lanthorn • Martin • Middle • St Thomas's • Salt
• Wakefield • Wardrobe [remains] • Well • White [the oldest]

Over the centuries, the expanse, shape and style of the
fortress have changed many times, but William's castle has
always been at its heart. Work began on building a new tower in
stone – the White Tower – with walls 15ft thick, about a decade
later (with the citizenry of London less than happy about being
conscripted as cheap labour). At its highest point the walls are
90ft tall, with sheer sides designed to make climbing difficult,
and tiny windows with angled frames to allow the least access

to incoming missiles. Each corner is reinforced with turrets: two square ones on the western side, a semi-circular projection at the south-eastern corner, which forms the apse of the Chapel Royal of St John the Evangelist, and a tower housing the main stairs at the north-eastern corner.

This was the structure that would become known as the White Tower, and it echoes both the position and the design of William's keep in his Norman capital, Rouen. Although unusual in England at the time, this style of building had been favoured by French kings for almost 100 years, and evidence suggests the White Tower may have been modelled on the castle at Ivry la Bataille, near Evreux, in Normandy.

William didn't live to see the fortress completed, and it was finished by his second son, William Rufus (1087-1100), who succeeded him. We do know that in 1100 William Rufus imprisoned his former adviser, Ranulf Flambard, there, so it was presumably considered a secure keep. However, since Ranulf went on to become the Tower's first escapee (see Chapter 6), perhaps it wasn't all that secure after all.

Most of the information we have about later monarchs' alterations and improvements to the Tower comes from the

---

The **Chapel Royal of St Peter ad Vincula**
[in chains] gets its name from St Peter's imprisonment
in Jerusalem by King Herod. The present-day chapel
dates from the 16th century, but a chapel probably
existed here from the very earliest Norman times.
Today, it is the parish church of the Tower.

royal accounts rolls, which fill in some but not all of the picture. So we know, for example, that Henry I (1100-1135) spent money on the Tower, but precisely on what is uncertain. The Wardrobe Tower, east of the White Tower, could have been the result of his work, or he could have spent the money on lodgings, workshops or domestic buildings around the keep, or on what became known as the King's Houses, the expanding royal apartments.

Richard the Lionheart (1189-1199) spent almost no time at any of his English castles – he was far too busy doing battle against the infidel in the Crusades – but he did instruct his chief minister, William Longchamp, Bishop of Ely and Constable at the Tower, to undertake dramatic construction work. In 1190, the year he left for the Crusades, Richard's remodelling of the Tower's defences cost about twice as much as the sum needed to build a new, average-sized castle. Unfortunately, very little of what he did remains. We do know that a large ditch was dug to the north, a 'moat of great depth' according to contemporary chronicler Roger of Howden, enclosing a new bailey about twice the size of the original. The polygonal Bell Tower was also built around this period, and the wall enclosing the bailey was extended and probably strengthened, although this may have been done during the reign of Richard's brother, John (1199-1216).

Even before coming to the throne, John provided a first test of Richard's new reinforcements by laying siege to the Tower in 1191 (there was little love lost between the brothers). William Longchamp wasn't able to hold the keep for long, not because of the difficulty of defending it, but because he had been surprised and only had food for a few days in store. After just three days he surrendered. Having built one of the best defended castles in Europe it seems a little remiss to forget to provision it.

As ruler, John spent considerable periods at the Tower, and had stone-throwing devices, probably catapults or trebuchets, installed, as well as palisades erected to further strengthen the defences. By the time his young son, Henry III (1216-1272), came to the throne, however, the Tower was no longer in the king's hands. Most of the nobility had been in revolt against his father, and the previous year they had taken the Tower and installed in residence there the French Dauphin, Louis, whom they had hoped to place on the throne. Only after a year of fighting did the forces of a 10-year-old Henry defeat those of Louis, at the Battle of Lincoln in 1217.

Henry III was not the most effective ruler, but he is remembered as an ambitious builder. The layout of the Tower as we recognise it today, with its pentagonal bailey and the White Tower towards the centre of it, owes a great deal to this king, who reigned for 56 years.

The Tower's defences, however, must have seemed in good condition, because Henry concentrated at first on refurbishing the royal apartments and extending the buildings given over to the royal court. As well as almost completely rebuilding the Chapel Royal of St Peter ad Vincula, and adding fine stained glass windows and decorations to the interior of the Chapel of St John in the White Tower, Henry developed an area on the riverside of the fortress known today as the Medieval Palace.

In 1503, **the body of Elizabeth of York,** wife of Henry VII, lay in state in the **Chapel Royal of St John the Evangelist** after her death in the Tower during childbirth.

But the change Henry instigated that probably made the most impact on how we perceive the Tower was cosmetic, not structural. In March 1240 he ordered the central keep to be whitewashed inside and out, in what was then the newfangled European fashion. The gleaming whitewash has long since disappeared, but the name of the White Tower has stuck.

It wasn't until the 1230s that Henry turned to the fortifications, reinforcing the old inner ward with massive stone walls, parts of which survive today, and building the Coldharbour Gate leading to the White Tower. (Although this gate was demolished in 1675-76, its foundations can still be seen.) In addition, Henry hugely expanded the land enclosed by the castle, extending the curtain wall along the river another 50ft or so beyond the original Roman wall and then building the Salt Tower to reinforce it. He also extended to the north, adding two huge D-shaped towers to the wall as he went – the Broad Arrow Tower and the Constable Tower – culminating in the Martin Tower at the far northern end. These towers provided extra lodgings in their upper rooms, and ideal vantage points from their lower ones for the garrison to fire on any attackers foolish enough to approach the wall – their bulging shape allowed archers to fire parallel to the line of the walls all the way along.

New ramparts were built across from the Martin Tower, reinforced with three even taller D-shaped towers. These, the Brick, Bowyer and Flint Towers, were built tall because the ground beyond them rose up, and those defending the castle needed to still be able to fire down on approaching attackers.

Finally, a new moat was dug. Moats had been dug around the Tower before, with little success: either they silted up or they emptied when the Thames (still tidal this far downstream) retreated. This time, a Flemish engineer called John 'le Fossur' – 'the ditcher' – appears to have succeeded. His efforts resulted in an expanse of water 160ft wide in certain spots, with dams to keep the water in place at all levels of the tides.

The moat we see today is its successor, completed in 1281 when Edward I (1272-1307) had a new, more extensive curtain wall built. Edward filled it with pike, to provide a ready source of fish for Friday consumption, although how tasty they were is debatable, given that all the Tower's waste went into the moat too – an unhygienic process that continued until the 1840s.

As his massive building works continued through the final 30 years of his reign, Henry had only one problem – people believed they were haunted. And haunted by no less a personage than Thomas Becket, the Archbishop of Canterbury, who had been murdered on the orders of Henry's grandfather, Henry II (1154-1189). As one particular

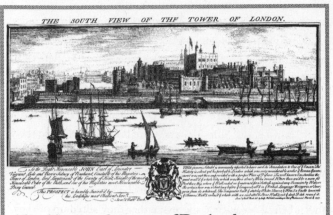

THE SOUTH VIEW OF THE TOWER OF LONDON.

The kings and queens of England often only ever stayed at the **Tower of London** for a few days at a time. Moving from household to household around the country was a useful way of keeping an eye on what troublemakers were up to. Some rulers led such peripatetic lifestyles that, on average, they moved on every three to four days.

gateway tower was being erected it crumbled 'as if struck by an earthquake,' according to a contemporary report, on the evening of 23 April, St George's Day. That same night the ghost of Thomas Becket appeared to a priest in London and told him the tower would fall again on St George's Day. The king ordered it rebuilt, with thicker walls and sturdier materials, but exactly a year later 'the walls which had been built around the Tower collapsed irreparably'. Excavations near the Beauchamp Tower uncovered timbers in the 1990s that have been dated to 1240 or 1241, which may have been the remains of this construction.

The Tower is said to be one of the most haunted places on earth. Reported sightings include:

The Sallyport, near the West Gate – The modern gas fire turning into a blazing hearth flanked by two Tudor guards.

Tower Hill – A procession of Medieval guards and the Sheriff of the Tower carrying a severed head on a pike.

Tower Green – The extremely active executee Margaret Pole on the anniversary of her death.

Traitor's Gate – Two Tudor women, accompanied by Yeoman Warders, passing through the gate.

Audience Chamber, Wakefield Tower – Henry VI pacing up and down at midnight on the 21 May.

The Bloody Tower – Edward V and his younger brother, Richard, haunting the spot where they are said to have been disposed of by Richard III.

The White Tower – A figure known as the White Lady, sometimes identified with Anne Boleyn, standing in a window.

Salt Tower – Several Yeoman Warders have reported feelings of being sat on and suffocated when resting in the guardroom.

Yeoman Warder's Flat in the Martin Tower – A woman called Mary and a bear so terrifying it's supposed to have frightened a guard to death around the turn of the century.

Constable Tower – A friendly ghost, who smells of saddle soap and likes to turn up whenever the staff living there are celebrating something.

On his return from the Crusades, Henry's son, Edward I, set about completing and adding to his father's work. The inner parts of the Tower precincts have undergone much change since, but the great outer defences we see today are largely Edward's fortress palace.

Edward raised an even more extensive curtain wall and within that, at the north-east and north-west corners, built two bastions, known as Legge's Mount and Brass Mount, from which archers could cover the moat as well as the high ground of Tower Hill. He also extended out into the river on the south side, creating what we now call Water Lane. Importantly, he shifted the main entrance to the south-west corner so that arrivals, whether friend or foe, had to traverse a double-gated walkway to the D-shaped Lion Tower (which no longer survives), built in a large basin of water formed by extending the moat, and then move along a thin causeway overlooked by a pair of forbidding, fortified towers, the Middle Tower and the Byward Tower. A masterpiece of unwelcoming architecture.

A DEFENSIVE FORTRESS

For the duration of the Hundred Years War, which dragged on until the middle of the 15th century, the Tower became a major centre for the storage and supply of arms, armour and heavy weaponry. Storage space was at a premium, and even rooms formerly used by kings, such as Edward I's chamber in St Thomas's Tower, began to fill up with armaments.

As well as supporting the English Army in France, the Tower was periodically having to provide shelter from

To enable supplies for the **army fighting in France** to be dispatched easily, a wharf was built from the Tower out into the **Thames**. Such were the escalating demands of the war that the wharf had to be extended no less than three times. Supervising the final extension, between 1389 and 1391, was a then-unknown civil servant, **Geoffrey Chaucer.**

aggression nearer home. In 1381, Wat Tyler led the Peasants' Revolt, when a mob of peasants marched on London. They were protesting at the imposition of one tax too many to fund the seemingly endless war. Richard II (1377-1399) and his family had to take refuge in the Tower when sympathisers let the rebels into the city and they attacked various royal homes. No one quite knows how, but several hundred of the 20,000 rebels managed to penetrate the Tower's supposedly impregnable defences, where they ran wild, 'liberated' some weapons (see Chapter 2), tried to kiss the king's mother and, more seriously, killed the Archbishop of Canterbury.

Richard II was again forced to take refuge in the Tower at Christmas 1387, when the country was in a state of unrest and his lords in revolt. Finally, in 1399, he lost his battle to keep the crown – confiscating the lands of Henry Bolingbroke, son of Edward III's third son, John of Gaunt (supposedly the richest man in the country), had been a step too far. Bolingbroke raised an army abroad and invaded England, forced Richard, again in the Tower, to abdicate, and had himself crowned within six months. Bolingbroke, now Henry IV (1399-1413), would have to rely on the Tower for protection when the late King Richard's supporters made an attempt to overthrow him.

Henry IV's seizure of the throne led to a long dynastic war between descendants of two of Edward III's sons: Edmund, Duke of York (family symbol: a white rose) and John of Gaunt, Duke of Lancaster (family symbol: a red rose). The Wars of the Roses embroiled the Tower in one of its saddest and most famous tales: The Princes in the Tower (see Chapter 6).

But the nature of war was changing. The Yorkist Edward IV (1461-1470 and 1471-1483) was fighting in the first days of the gun, and his main addition to the Tower, a brick-walled yard protecting the western entrance, was specially designed for guns to be mounted and to withstand returning fire. He also had makeshift earthworks, in the form of barrels filled with earth, banked along the wharf and gun emplacements set on them – a rough and ready defence, but they did work when the Tower came under bombardment from ships in the river.

This was the last time the Tower was to come under fire (apart from one bomb that landed ineffectually in the moat in World War I) until World War II.

HOME AND COUNTRY

The Tower was very effective as a deterrent and symbol of power, and reasonably effective as a fortress – even if its defences have been breached several times in its history – but how did it fare as a home?

As a royal keep, the White Tower was one of the largest of its kind, clearly built with habitation as well as war in mind.

During **World War II**, the Tower of London was hit several times by V-rockets and incendiary bombs. The Main Guard, Hospital Block and North Bastion were destroyed, but the older parts of the Tower survived surprisingly well. After all, they had been built to withstand close-range pounding from **Medieval siege engines**.

Its rooms were provided with ample fireplaces from the earliest construction, and latrines were even built into the outer walls. The dark basement provided plenty of room for storage and there is evidence of a reinforced space specially built to house the king's treasures (see Chapter 5). The basement also contained a well, possibly the most vital feature of any keep which was designed to withstand lengthy sieges and had to have its own reliable water supply.

There were two further floors (another floor and a new, raised roof were added around the 15th century), the lower one reached by an exterior wooden staircase – again a good precaution against forced entrance, because it could be broken down or burnt to hinder the enemy. Once inside, the other levels were linked via a spiral staircase, again a defensive precaution. A spiral staircase gave right-handed defenders (which almost all were) an advantage when wielding a weapon.

Each level of the White Tower had a main room over 100ft long on the west side. The larger windows and access to the magnificent Chapel suggest that the second floor contained the king's main Audience Chamber. It was common in palaces from the 11th and 12th centuries for the most important person to occupy the higher floor, while their retainers would be quartered below, where they could effectively protect them from attack.

Most of the early improvements to the Tower and its environs were made to increase its strength and effectiveness as a fortress, but from the 13th century there are real signs of building for comfort. Henry III is known to have had the story of Antioch painted on the walls of the royal apartments and he decorated the large Great Hall, measuring 80 x 50ft, with arched timber arcades. At the western end of this hall, in the Lanthorn Tower, lay the Queen's apartments, where Henry's wife, Eleanor of Provence, had her rooms fashionably whitewashed and painted with lines to make the interior walls look like they were formed from large cut stones.

Despite all of these home comforts, Henry III actually used the Palace of Westminster as his major London residence, the Tower was just for occasional visits. Even so, he was the first royal of record to landscape the area and create gardens, including a vineyard and an orchard to the north of the castle. Edward I had a new water gate (which came to be known later as Traitor's Gate) built in the form of St Thomas's Tower, so that he could arrive by barge and disembark closer to his chambers. The building was embellished with fine tracery in the stained glass windows, and painted statuary on the rooftops.

The royal apartments were richly decorated by the standard of the day, with many soft furnishings and hangings, although few seats had backs. Beds, on the other hand, were designed with high backs. People preferred to sleep in a sitting position, propped up on cushions, lying down was for those near death.

Everything, from the royal bed to the meanest water jug, would have been crafted by hand and decorated. Each carpet was hand-knotted, each hanging the result of hundreds of hours of hand-stitching. Much of the wooden surfaces, whether carved or plain, would have been decorated with bright colours, with still more patterns featured on the floor tiles. Designs often included heraldic badges and standards, or featured animals and plants, often with symbolic meaning. Gilding with paper-thin sheets of gold added gleaming highlights to the already complex colour schemes.

Edward III (1327-1377) also engaged in wholesale repairs and improvements to the Tower, including constructing the Cradle Tower – as private access to the royal apartments, with a snug guard room downstairs – and the Develin Tower. Where the Queen's House now stands, he is thought to have had the Constable's House rebuilt, as well as making substantial alterations to the Great Hall. Henry VII (1485-1509) built a

---

In the Middle Ages, those who were to be knighted by the monarch before a coronation spent the night before receiving the accolade in fasting and prayer in the Chapel Royal of St John the Evangelist at the Tower. Part of this vigil involved a ritualistic bath as a sign of purification. There is an account of this ceremony in the reign of King Henry IV, and it continued until the mid-17th century. George I re-established the Order of the Bath in 1725.

---

new tower, a gallery and a new garden, while before the coronation of Anne Boleyn in 1533, Henry VIII (1509-1547) refurbished the public rooms and those to be used by his new queen – some needed new floors and roofs, an indication of their age.

The Tower continued to be used as a royal palace, albeit only for short periods at a time, up until the reign of Elizabeth I (1558-1603), but after Henry VIII's death, the Tower was really only used symbolically by the monarch. Probably because she had been imprisoned there during the reign of her half-sister Mary (1553-1558), Elizabeth I understandably did not favour the Tower as a residence.

By the time James I (1603-1625) arrived from Scotland to accept the English throne, the royal palace at the Tower was full of leaky pipes and rotten ceilings and the Medieval Great Hall was a shell. In order to hold his coronation celebrations, the king had to have a temporary wood and canvas structure hastily erected inside the Hall so that the dilapidation was hidden.

The Tower's small chambered towers and medieval stone construction must have seemed increasingly outdated and austere to later Tudors and Stuarts and their sucessors. Its days as a royal residence were over.

However, as John Stow recorded in 1590, life at the Tower had never been livelier or more vital: 'This tower is a Citadell, to defend or commaund the Citie: a ryall place for assemblies, and treaties. A Prison of estate, for the most dangerous offenders, the onely place of coynage for all England at this time: the armourie for warlike provision: the

The monarch's customary procession from the Tower of London to Westminster Palace the day before the coronation dates back to the 14th century and to the coronation of Richard II. With the exception of James I and Charles I, whose processions were cancelled because of the plague, this tradition continued up until the reign of James II. James replaced the Vigil Procession, as it was known, with a walking procession from Westminster Hall to Westminster Abbey on the day of the coronation. Today, the sovereign is driven by carriage from Buckingham Palace to Westminster Abbey.

Treasurie of the ornaments and jewels of the crowne, and generall conserver of the most Records of the Kings Courts of Justice at Westminster.'

The business of running the country was performed by a comparatively small number of people, but the Tower itself was ever-busy, fulfilling numerous functions. Increasingly, the Tower of London was seen, according to historian Raphael Holinshed, as an 'armourie and house of munition'. Not to mention a mint, a zoo, a treasure trove and the most famous prison in the land.

CHAPTER

ARMS & ARMOUR

When the opening of the Royal Armouries Museum in Leeds hit the headlines in 1996, many people feared that the Tower of London was losing one of its major attractions. After all, its collection of arms and armour constituted the oldest museum in the country, and one of the oldest in the world. But the White Tower still retains a magnificent armoury of pieces, most with direct connection to the Tower itself, including numerous early weapons – pikes, halberds, maces, axes and the like – a rather striking display of horse armour, and a splendid suit of armour belonging to Henry VIII, as well as armour worn by Charles I (1625-1649), Charles II (1660-1685) and James II (1685-1688) and a suit believed to be the largest in the world: its owner would have been 6ft 9in tall.

The Tower became a repository for armour very early on in its life. From the 12th century, all the royal possessions were looked after by a department called the Chamber (named after the king's private chamber), which took care not only of clothing and jewels, but also everything from food and drink to furniture and weapons. All possessions that were too large to travel around with the monarch would be stored at the Tower and the king would send for particular items and have them transported to wherever they were needed. By around 1230, a sub-department, the Wardrobe, had developed into an independent organisation, and by 1253 had evolved into the

Nothing remains of the Medieval arsenal, as **Henry VIII** had the Tower restocked with up-to-date weapons of war.

Great Wardrobe, which later produced a further offshoot, the Privy Wardrobe. It was the Privy Wardrobe that was responsible for all of the king's arms and armour.

WILL SOMMERS'S ARMOUR.

.s preserved in the tower of London ...
..h as the Act directly I Herbert Pall Mall 1 June 1794 ..

During the following century, the Great Wardrobe, concerned with clothes and furniture, was eventually moved out into the city, but as the Hundred Years War progressed, the Privy Wardrobe was used more and more as a supply armoury and a store for captured enemy arms. The Privy Wardrobe at this time was run by men with a great thirst for power (which pretty much equated with floorspace within the crowded precincts of the Tower), and they embraced the role of overseeing the storage of arms and armour as the best route to fulfilling their ambitions. Under their control, the Tower's Privy Wardrobe became the largest store of weaponry in the country and the nation's main military supply base. This was a crucial function when you consider that Britain had no standing army until 1661.

Despite the amount of weaponry stored there, the Tower of London was rarely strongly defended, its very structure was deemed impregnable. During the Peasants' Revolt in

1381, the excited army of farmhands and villagers managed to get into the Privy Wardrobe, where they killed the Archbishop of Canterbury. They also stole 110 mail coats, 900 bows and two cannons. However, the rebels overlooked the need for shot or gunpowder, so their prize booty proved largely of little use to them!

With the responsibility for, firstly, personal and then national armour and weaponry, there evolved a number of offices connected with its upkeep. Even as early as 1275, during the reign of Edward I, the rolls of court business record wages being paid to the King's Armourer and to the Master of the King's Crossbows and Bolts.

As well as a resident staff of armourers, the Privy Wardrobe called in specialists when they needed them. In the late-14th century, Richard Davy, a highly skilled maker of breastplates 'who has lived in Lombardy', was called to the Tower 'for the purpose of making them for the king's use and instructing others therein.' The Lombardy connection was of value because, at this time, Italian armour was considered superior, so Richard Davy's knowledge would have been highly sought after.

There was also a King's Smith, paid for by the Treasury, who made repairs and manufactured new pieces for the monarch as required. Master Walter the Smith is recorded as making 'engines of war' that were used by Edward III at the Battle of Crécy in 1346.

By the time of Crécy, gunpowder was being manufactured in quantity at the Tower, and before the century was out the stores of bows and arrows kept at the Tower were beginning to decrease as firearms, unreliable and perilous to use as they were, became the new fighting weapons of choice. A sub-department responsible for the gunnery already existed by 1370, and John Derby is listed as the *clericus pro officio gunnorum regis* – Clerk of the Office of the King's Guns. Most firearms would have been manufactured by the Armoury's smith, but there were also specialist craftsmen who constructed and repaired the cannons under the direction of the Keeper of the Wardrobe. Randolph Hatton, who was Keeper of the Wardrobe from 1382 to 1396, purchased 73 new cannons from William Woodward's foundry during his period in office.

In 1414, the first Master of the Ordnance, Nicholas Merbury, was appointed. This marked a theoretical division between the Armoury, which dealt with armour and weapons for hand-to-hand combat, and the Ordnance, which covered firearms and the larger equipment of war. However, in reality, their functions seemed fairly fluid. The Master of the Ordnance and the Master of the Armoury were two of the most eminent figures at the Tower, and the division was, inevitably, an opportunity for power-play and political manoeuvring. There are records of the Ordnance handling orders for swords and bladed weapons, suggesting it was a

---

We may view him in a different light today, but 300 years ago **Henry VIII** was – almost literally – a touchstone of fertility. In the 18th century, women would queue to stick pins into the codpieces of Henry's **suits of armour** in the belief that it would guarantee they would bear children.

very active, and possibly more efficient department – and probably one keen to dominate. In time, the Armoury lessened in power and influence as guns and cannon became the major tools of war, and on the death of William Legge, Master of the Armouries in 1671, the Master of the Ordnance officially took over the duties of both posts.

A WORKING ARSENAL

Despite Henry VIII having an extensive new building erected for his clothes and personal belongings, space for the Armoury at the Tower remained tight. Right at the start of Elizabeth I's reign, a period during which the Tower was particularly full of prisoners, the Lieutenant of the Tower and Captain of the Mint suggested that the Armoury should be moved to 'the Great Mill erected by My Brooke' (a disused Medieval water mill) near Traitor's Gate. Six years later, however, two new Armouries seem to have been formed for small arms and artillery, located in the White Tower itself. Then, in 1580, the Treasury received estimates for 'making rooms within the Great White Tower... for placing and hanging up all of the Armour'. Nothing seems to have been done instantly, but in 1595, a Swiss traveller, Joseph Platter, wrote about quantities of armour being kept in the White Tower.

The Board of Ordnance gradually took over the White Tower. For much of its life the Board's job was to oversee a working arsenal, not only was it responsible for arming Britain's armies, but also for designing and testing new weapons during a period of unprecedented conquest and empire-building.

'We were next led into the Armoury, in which are these particularities: – Spears, out of which you may shoot; shields, that will give fire four times; a great many rich halberds, commonly called partisans, with which the guard defend the royal person in battle; some lances, covered with red and green velvet, and the  body-armour of Henry VIII; many and very beautiful arms, as well for men as for horses in horse-fights; the lance of Charles Brandon, Duke of Suffolk, three spans thick; two pieces of cannon, the one fires three, the other seven balls at a time; two others made of wood, which the English has at the siege of Boulogne, in France […] nineteen cannon of a thicker make than ordinary, and in a room apart; thirty-six of a smaller; other cannon for chain-shot; and balls proper to bring down masts of ships. Cross-bows, bows and arrows, of which to this day the English make great use in their exercises; but who can relate all that is to be seen here? Eight or nine men employed by the year are scarce sufficient to keep all the arms bright.'

Paul Hentzner, *Travels in England during the reign of Queen Elizabeth*, 1598

The expanding empire had its own effect on the Armoury's collection. As British influence spread across the globe, more and more ethnic militaria was sent back to the home shores, either as spoils of war or as gifts from foreign rulers. The Tower became a repository for arms and armour from all around the world, from finely wrought Japanese samurai swords to a complete suit of armour for an elephant.

Emphasis slowly began to shift in the 19th century towards preserving an accurate history of the country's military achievements. Curiosities and magpie selections were out and educational displays were in. The Tower began to purchase with the intention of creating the greatest history of arms and armour in the world.

VISITING THE ARMS

One of the earliest accounts of tourist interest in the Armoury comes from the late-15th century, when Wilwold von Schaumburg, a visiting knight, was impressed by the various pieces of militaria he was shown. From this time on, showing off the Tower's weaponry to foreign dignitaries became a way of displaying the extent of England's arsenal. During Elizabeth I's reign, distinguished gentlemen as well as diplomats sought and succeeded in gaining access to the collections, no doubt going away impressed by this evidence of the country's might. What they mostly saw was 'modern' Tudor arms and armour, because the young Henry VIII, in a bellicose mood, had ordered all the older items cleared out of the Tower to make way for the new machinery of war he

> The current display of suits of armour contains one tiny set, made for someone under 3ft tall. It has been variously identified as armour made for Richard, Duke of York, one of the Princes in the Tower, and Sir Jeffrey Hudson, the dwarf who entertained Charles I's queen, Henrietta Maria.

was having made. However, not all visitors to the Armoury were overawed. Jacob Rathgeb, secretary to the Duke of Wurttemberg, toured the Armoury in 1592 and found it 'full of dust' and 'confusion and disorder'.

Jubilation at the return of Charles II and the restoration of the monarchy in 1660 provided the impetus to create a public museum that would celebrate Britain's military achievements. The fledgling museum was certainly not short of artefacts to display – at one point, the Small Armoury held armaments for up to 100,000 soldiers.

The Armouries are called just that because they began as four different displays in the 17th century: The Spanish Armoury, The Line of Kings, The Small Armoury and The Artillery Room.

The Spanish Armoury – A bit of a misnomer this, because the Spanish Armoury was certainly not Spanish. It was a collection of rather fearsome objects that were supposed to represent booty from wrecked ships of the Spanish Armada when it attempted to invade England during Elizabeth I's reign, in 1588. In fact, the only items from the actual Armada ever thought to have been sent to the Tower are two cannons. On later examination, most pieces in the collection were found to be early Tudor, predating the Armada by at least 50 years.

Most people believed the Spanish Armoury collection at least originated in Spain, but even this was not true. In reality, it was made up of all sorts of items already in the Tower's possession, including a number of instruments of torture which were described with great liveliness in the early guides to the collection that appeared in the 18th century.

When war with Spain broke out again in 1779, the collection was expanded by adding an inspiring figure of Elizabeth I mounted on horseback, recreating the stirring moment of her speech at Tilbury Docks, when she declared that she had 'the heart of a woman, but the stomach of a king'.

The collection's name was changed to Queen Elizabeth's Armoury in 1837, when the ever-correct Samuel Meyrick (see page 39) pointed out a majority of the contents were too old to have been part of the Armada's armaments. (This makes you wonder why it wasn't renamed the King Henry VIII Armoury, given that it included his magnificent collection of personal armour and weapons.)

The collection was originally displayed in the House of Ordnance built to the north of the White Tower. When this

> 'The Government should [not] have allowed a paltry building like that of the New Horse Armory to have been erected against the venerable and noble White Tower.'
>
> *Thomas Allen, author of the* History and Antiquities of London, *1827, was not a fan of the neo-gothic home of the Armoury at the Tower.*

For many years, **William the Conqueror** was displayed in the Line of Kings wielding a musket, which was not invented until some 300 years after he died!

was demolished in 1688, it moved to a storehouse erected to the north of the Wakefield Tower. In 1837, the collection was moved again, to the crypt of St John's Chapel in the White Tower, where it remained throughout Queen Victoria's reign.

The Line of Kings – This series of life-size models of the various monarchs and some of their most famous knights, mounted on horseback, was first created at Greenwich during the reign of Henry VIII. The display was moved to the Tower for safety during the Civil War, and then, at the time of the restoration of the monarchy, was deemed a perfect vehicle to reinforce the desirability of kingship.

The Line of Kings proved to be one of the Tower's most popular early tourist attractions, even if it was hardly historically accurate. It was originally assembled with more consideration given to spectacle than accuracy, and most of the models, irrespective of when they reigned, were clad in 16th-century armour and carried contemporary weapons. The Line also blithely omitted figures whose claim to the throne was unpopular or dubious, such as Richard III and Edward II. After its arrival at the Tower, the Board of Ordnance set about updating the collection with great vigour. The refurbished Line, unveiled in 1685, included a fine figure of Charles II made by the great wood carver Grinling Gibbons and sculptor John Nost. Charles I was added the following year.

The Line of Kings was initially squeezed into the House of Ordnance with the Spanish Armada collection, but moved to the first floor of the New Armouries building to the south-east of the White Tower, while 17 newly made horses were provided for the models, and the kings and knights were posed in a long procession along one side of the room. Figures of famous courtiers such as John of Gaunt were gathered along the other side. William III (1689-1702) was added promptly after his death in 1702, but George I (1714-1727) had to wait until 1750, 23 years after he died, and he is represented not by a full equestrian figure, but as a bronze head sculpted by John Cheer. The final king to be added to the Line was George II (1727-1760), in 1768.

The display was supposed to be very lifelike – a little too lifelike on one memorable occasion. A surviving letter from a George Follett to a Robert Harley on 8 September 1692 describes an unusual effect when a small earthquake shook London while he was at the Tower: 'Amongst the effects of the late Earthquake was something comical. You remember the large new store house at the Tower and there above stairs all the heroes and their horses are set forth in armour. Suffering such a shock it was great prowess in them to stand their ground; but the mortals thereabouts, conceiving by the clashing of their armour that they were upon the march, gave instances of the two extremities of motion.'

Verisimilitude of the historical line-up was finally addressed in 1826, when Samuel Rush Meyrick was appointed its

Samuel Rush Meyrick, a scholar of arms and armour who was invited to rearrange the collection at the Tower, was a colourful and controversial figure. His father and grandfather had built up the family fortune as army supply agents, and from them he learned his love of martial accoutrements. He also became enamoured of all things Welsh, he claimed descent, with no real justification, from Sir Gelly Meyrick, a Welsh adventurer and friend of the Earl of Essex who had wound up on the scaffold in 1601. Samuel's elopement at the age of 20 with a young Welsh girl led to his being cut out of his father's will, but he earned a living as a lawyer and writer, while amassing a large collection of armour. In a search for a suitable setting for his collection, he lighted upon Goodrich Castle on the Welsh borders, but the owner refused to sell to him. He responded in what seems rather a spiteful gesture by building Goodrich Court nearby, in an over-the-top Gothic style apparently designed to out-do her in the grand homes stakes.

custodian. A keen Medievalist and widely-published historian, Meyrick had first come to the attention of George IV (1820-1830) because of his personal collection of armour, and he used to advise theatre producers and artists on the accuracy of their props. He was awarded the Royal Guelphic Order in 1832 for his contributions to the Tower's Armouries.

Meyrick supervised the moving of the line into a new home in the New Horse Armoury, a controversial Gothic construction that had been recently added to the Tower. (It was pulled down in 1883, having attracted censure throughout its brief 60-year life within the Tower precincts – the historian Thomas Allen railed against the 'paltry building' having been allowed to be erected against the 'venerable and noble White Tower'.)

From the New Horse Armoury, the Armoury collections moved back to the White Tower where they have remained to this day, gradually filling the whole space and spilling over.

The Small Armoury and the Artillery Room –

These two collections are sometimes spoken of as one, because they both occupied the Grand Storehouse. The ground floor of the Storehouse housed the Royal Train of Artillery, with both modern guns and historic trophies ranged along the sides of the rooms, ornately gilded and painted ceremonial gun carriages on show alongside artillery drums. There was also, astonishing for the era, a wooden diving bell, kept largely as a curiosity rather than as a practical military vehicle.

Most of the weaponry in the Small Armoury was held on the first floor in 16 huge chests, but what this part of the Armouries collection became famous for were the wall tableaux created in the 1690s by John Harris. Harris built up entire scenes and complex patterns constructed exclusively from thousands of swords, pistols and bayonets – visitors could marvel at rising and setting suns, a three-dimensional organ, a pair of gates and, most strikingly, a hydra-like multi-headed mythical beast which, it was said 'no one ever beheld without Astonishment'.

He went on to make similarly unusual uses of weapons at Hampton Court and Windsor Castle (which still remain), and although Harris's originals haven't survived at the Tower, there is a reconstruction of his fascinating form of art.

The Grand Storehouse was destroyed by fire in 1841, a conflagration which burned from 10pm on 30 October until 7am the next morning. The Train of Artillery had been transferred to Woolwich some years previously, but the Small Armoury collection was completely destroyed. Twisted bits of metal and charred arms were sold to members of the public as historic souvenirs, sometimes for up to £1 (around £64.79 in modern terms). The Waterloo Barracks now stands where the Grand Storehouse was once, both a vital link to the country's defences and a treasure trove of weaponry.

This wasn't the last time the collection would suffer damage. On 24 January 1885, a bomb exploded on the first floor of the White Tower. Despite being timed to go off on a

---

Mons Meg, the famous 15th-century cannon at Edinburgh Castle, that is supposed to have been made at **Mons in Flanders,** was kept at the Tower of London after it was pinched by the English in 1754, following the quelling of the final Jacobite rebellion. It was only restored to Scotland in 1829.

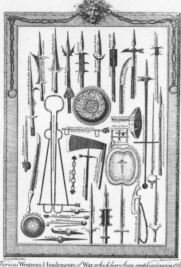

Various Weapons & Implements of War which have been employed against the ENGLISH by different Enemies Now deposited in the TOWER of London

(Plate from Skinner's *History of London*, 1795.)

busy Saturday afternoon, when the Tower would have been crowded with visitors, no one was seriously injured and little damage was done. More serious was the attack made on 17 July 1974, which killed one woman, a librarian called Dorothy Household, and injured 41 others. A bomb is thought to have been put in one of the cannons. The bomb was believed to have been placed there by the IRA, who were also suspected of a bombing at the Houses of Parliament a week earlier. One witness later remembered: 'I actually thought someone had fired a cannon.'

RECORDING HISTORY

One of the key figures in the history of the Armoury is Robert Porrett, Chief Clerk in the early years of the reign of Queen Victoria (1837-1901). A Fellow of the Royal Society and the Society of Antiquaries, Porrett persuaded the Board of Ordnance to start buying up important pieces of military history and recruited John Hewitt, a well-regarded antiquarian, to join his staff. It was Hewitt who published the first truly informative book on the Royal Armouries, *The*

Tower: Its Histories, Armories and Antiquities, in 1841, so at least we have a detailed record of what was lost in the fire that autumn night. (The first full catalogue appeared in 1859, and the standard reference work today dates back nearly 100 years, to 1916, and was put together by the then Curator, Charles Ffoulkes.)

Porrett and Hewitt did a great deal to preserve and develop the Armoury collections from a professional historian's viewpoint, but they also made a significant contribution to the popularity of the museum, thanks to a dramatically successful experiment with entrance fees.

As with most of the collections in the Tower, the Armouries were regarded in the 18th and early-19th centuries as amusements for the rich only – tourism wasn't for the poor: they neither had the money, time nor energy for it. However, with the advent of better standards of living, larger city populations, mechanisation and increased transport facilities, this meant that the Tower museums were increasingly within the range and the pocket of a burgeoning Victorian middle class, who did have the time and the desire to go sightseeing. Reducing entrance fees brought them flocking, and visitor numbers increased by almost eight-fold in two years.

In 1837 it cost 2s to see **the Armoury,** a sum which 11,104 people paid. The next year the fee was halved, and halved again in 1839. As a result, 84,872 people visited the museum that year, and even though each visitor only paid 6d, in total the museum took an extra £456.

In the wake of Porrett and Hewitt, many eminent art and military historians have held the post of Curator over the years (although, amazingly, the post wasn't recognised as a full-time job – or salaried – until 1973). At the dawn of the 20th century, the Curator, the 17th Viscount Dillon, spearheaded a move to transfer the Royal Armouries collection to the British Museum. Viscount Dillon, who had an immense specialist knowledge of military antiquities, and also a penchant for trying on many of the collection's suits of armour, strongly believed the collection should be part of the British Museum, but just as he seemed to finally be winning the battle, the arrival of the Office of Works as controllers of the Tower in 1904 brought the scheme to a halt.

Probably on account of their immense size, the Royal Armouries were left in peace in their home in the White Tower for decades. But the collection grew faster, not more slowly, as it entered the 20th century, and began to outgrow even the White Tower. In 1988 the Armouries leased Fort Nelson, near Portsmouth, to house the overspill (this is now the home of the national collection of artillery), and in 1990, a new northern base of operations was unveiled in Leeds. When the Leeds Armouries opened, they allowed the collection in the Tower to focus, once more, on those ancient artefacts and wondrous displays our forefathers saw there.

CHAPTER

MENAGERIE

he collection of animals kept at the Tower of London used to be one of its most popular attractions. For many centuries the exotic and extraordinary animals kept in the Royal Menagerie were, in theory, only for the eyes of the sovereign and their guests, but in later years it became a popular tourist attraction.

The Royal Menagerie is thought to have been established at the Tower some time during the reign of King John. There are records of payments to animal keepers in 1210, but the collection may have started as early as 1204 when, during John's hasty retreat from the Norman territories he had been forced to relinquish, he shipped three boatloads of wild animals back to England.

His great-grandfather, Henry I, had begun collecting exotic species in 1125, which he kept at another royal palace, Woodstock, near Oxford – but it was John's successor, Henry III who really built up the collection. As a present to mark his wedding to Eleanor of Provence, he was given three leopards by his bride's brother, the Holy Roman Emperor Frederick II, reflecting the leopards on his standard (you can still see heraldic leopards decorating the royal apartments).

The historian Raphael Holinshed recorded in 1255: 'Lewis the French king, sent unto King Henrie, for a present, an Elephant, a beast most strange and wonderful to the English people, sith most seldome or neuer any of that kind had beene scene in England before that time.' (Charlemagne had an elephant in his collection as early as 801, given to him by Haroun al-Rashid, the Caliph of Baghdad.) Although Henry had a lavish house more than 40ft long built for the beast, it died of unknown causes within three years and was buried in the bailey. Its capacious quarters were later put to good use housing prisoners neither noble nor rich enough to warrant the more luxurious rooms (or even suites) available in the Tower.

But the story of England's first elephant doesn't end there. On 9 August 1258, the Constable of the Tower was ordered to dig it up and give the bones to the Sacrist of Westminster, possibly to be made into holy vessels, although there is no record of any carved elephant bone mounts or cups thereafter.

Thanks to an illustrated manuscript by historical writer Matthew Paris, scholars who didn't make it to London still got a chance to see pictures of marvels like the first elephant in Britain. Henry's elephant was depicted surprisingly accurately by Paris, who had clearly seen the beast for himself. In 1255 he wrote in his *Chronica Majora*: 'This was the only elephant ever seen in England, nor even in the countries on this side of the Alps; wherefore the

---

The keeping of exotic animals by princes and potentates can be traced back to Ancient Egypt. Queen Hatshepsut sent men across Africa to capture unusual species, which she then displayed as symbols of wealth and power, and traded with neighbouring rulers as long ago as 1490 BC. Four centuries later in China, Emperor Wen Wang of the Shang Dynasty created a 1,500-acre 'intelligence park' to display the widest possible range of plants and animals.

THE TOWER MENAGERIE ABOUT 1820.

'Access to these menageries was originally restricted to
friends of the owners and honoured guests,
but by the 17th century the public was admitted to some of
them on certain days, starting with the Tower of London,
and the Schonbrunn Palace in Vienna.'
'The Design of Zoos', *Architectural Science Review, vol 46*

people flocked together to see the novel sight.' His picture
provided several hitherto unknown details, such as the fact
that elephants do, in fact, have knee joints. Up until this
point, people believed pachyderms couldn't bend and that
they slept leaning up against trees.

Some of the animals that lived in the Royal Menagerie are
difficult to pin down. An 18th-century engraving depicts a
creature called a 'shah goest', which has never been identified

with any living species. In the picture it has some big cat qualities, but also the extended sinuousness of a ferret or stoat with what could be outsize horns or very long ears.

KEEPER OF THE LIONS

It was during the reign of Edward I that the official position Master of the King's Bears and Apes was created. With the addition of more big cats – a lion and lioness, leopard and two wild cats – during the 14th century, the role was transformed into Keeper of the Lions and Leopards.

By the 15th century, the Keeper of the King's Menagerie was pretty much an honorary title, bestowed by letters patent on people who had done the monarch a service. Henry VI gave the title to his steward, Thomas Rookes, and later to his favourite at the time, Ralph Hastings, while Richard III bestowed it to Sir Robert Brakenbury, who was at the same time Constable of the Tower and Master of the Mint. Under the later Tudor and Stuart monarchs, the Gill family, Essex landowners all, held the position for 113 years.

Prime Minister Robert Walpole used his influence to get a painter, John Ellys, the post of Keeper in 1739, in return for the assistance Ellys had given him in choosing and sourcing paintings. Walpole also managed to revive the practice of paying a daily allowance for upkeep of the animals, which had been phased out as income from charging visitors to view them grew. Ellys got 7s.6d (£44.80 in modern terms) a day, raised a couple of years later to 9s (£53.76 in modern terms) a day.

Who paid for the animals' upkeep was a continued source of contention. During the first few decades of the establishment of the Royal Menagerie, the king charged the Sheriffs of London and also of Bedford and Buckinghamshire with the task of covering the costs. A record for 23 March 1240 directs the Sheriff of London to provide for the King's lion and his keeper William (probably William de Botton). In 1244 the rate was set at 3 1/2d (£6.85 in modern terms) per day for lion and keeper, but by 1314 it had slipped back to just 1/2d (£0.73 in modern terms) a day for the keeper, and a quarter of a sheep for the lion to eat.

The polar bear, a gift from Norway, fared better, and the Sheriffs were ordered to pay 14d (£20.35 in modern terms) a day for him and his keeper, as well as providing money for chains and a muzzle – presumably they felt it was best to ensure there were adequate restraints for the animals!

What monarchs were willing to spend seemed to vary wildly. Edward III looked after his collection in style. His records for 1338 indicate an allowance of 12d (£26.76 in modern terms) a day for the keeper, as well as 2s.1d (£55.74 in modern terms) for the animals' upkeep – a significant sum which led to concerns from the Treasury about the size of the Menagerie. But 32 years later, William de la Garderobe was getting only 6d (£4.53 in modern terms) per day for each animal, and the same in wages. However, the Menagerie had expanded quite considerably by this time, so he earned almost £85 (around £15,000 in modern terms) during his nine-month tenure, which was a considerable income for the time.

REFURBISHING THE MENAGERIE

Although no Menagerie buildings remain, from at least the
1330s, the animals were probably housed in the Lion Tower,
close to the Middle Tower. For many years the cages were
simple wooden enclosures. In 1544, Pedro de Gante,
Secretary to the Duke of Najera, viewed the royal collection
and noted: 'Four lions, very large and fierce, and two
leopards, confined within wooden railings.'

The animals were kept in two-storey cages about 12ft
high, and displayed in the upper half during the day. At
night they were moved 'downstairs', so the upper cage could
be safely cleaned out. The first major improvements we
know about took place between 1604 and 1606, possibly
because of several gifts James I had received, including a
flying squirrel from Virginia, a tiger, a lioness, five camels
and an elephant. The two-tier wooden dens built around the
inside of the Lion Tower's ground floor were refurbished,
floors were relaid, channels sunk to allow waste to drain
away, and a safe exercise yard created with a 'great
cisterne... for the Lyons to drinke and washe themselfes in'.
The improvements also included a viewing platform 'for the
kinges Matie to stande on to see the Lyons lett out'.

> James I was such a fan of his lions, he designed a bottle with
> a nipple with which some orphaned lion cubs could be fed,
> and which he sent to the keeper with a note reading:
> 'I pray God your lordship an understand my description
> of a new engine to give a beast suck'.

It wasn't just watching the lions strolling around and stretching that interested King James. He was a big fan of animal baiting, and constructed a special pit at the Tower where he could view contests between lions and other beasts. A contemporary report notes that the exercise yard 'shall be maintayned and kept for speciall place to baight the Lyons with dogges, beares, bulles, bores etc', and Samuel Kiechel, who visited at the time, recorded the Menagerie contained 250 mastiffs, kept for this purpose. In 1936, during excavations around the Lion Tower, 18 mastiff skulls were dug up.

The Menagerie continued to expand, and was periodically refurbished, as the arrival of new species challenged the accommodation arrangements. In 1672 Christopher Wren began supervision of the new Lion House for the keeper by the south-east corner of the Lion Tower. The house had two storeys, plus attics and a cellar, and must have been substantial (the eventual cost was, precisely, £650.0s.6 3/4d, which in modern terms is equivalent to about £81,240). In 1694 a carpenter was paid for 'making up a new Denn between the owl cages and Leopards Denns in the Garden, for the beast called a Jana' (possibly a hyena, as one is advertised in 1697 as being in the collection).

'Henry was extremely fond of the wonders of distant countries, begging with great delight, as I have observed, from foreign kings, lions, leopards, lynxes, or camels – animals which England does not produce.'
William of Malmesbury notes Henry I's interest in exotic animals

A major innovation in 1777-78 was the introduction of 'fire flues', a primitive form of central heating which was 'carried through the Wild Beast's Dens to prevent them from Dying with Cold'. Perhaps the new heating also warmed the elephant, whose new house was being prepared in 1795. Renowned as long-lived animals, the Tower elephants seemed to die after only a few years.

In the 19th century safety became a greater consideration. Iron grilles were finally added to the fronts of the cages in 1802, and in 1810 Surveyor-General of the Works James Wyatt improved the lions' dens so that 'the animals cannot possibly escape, or get at each other'. Wyatt's design didn't allow for human error, however. His system of pulleys to open and shut doors, and make it easier to move large cats from one enclosure to another could be confusing, and in 1830 a junior keeper opened the wrong door at the wrong time, allowing a pair of tigers to come face to face with a lion: 'The roaring and the yelling of the combatants resounded through the yards, and excited in the various animals the most lively demonstrations of fear or rage.' Keepers eventually broke the fight up, but only by applying heated metal rods to the mouths and nostrils of the tigers. The lion, however, died of its wounds a few days later.

A SYMBOL OF POWER

For centuries menageries were regarded as a cross between living museums and symbols of power. If a ruler was master of lions and tigers, he or she was clearly fit to rule the country. By the reign of Elizabeth I, there had been lions at the Tower for centuries, and they were closely connected in the popular imagination with the continuation of the royal line. During Elizabeth's last illness, an old lioness at the Tower, also called Elizabeth, was reported to have pined and died, and similar events occurred towards the end of Charles II's life.

Much depended on the health and vigour of the Menagerie's animals, and they were looked after with great care, even if some of the information the keepers had about animal welfare was a little off the mark. But keeping wild beasts in a restricted environment like the Tower presented a huge challenge to the keepers, who knew little of animal medicine. The first elephant, as we have seen, lasted only three years, and in 1436, according to the *Chronicle of London*, 'deyde alle the lyons that weren the Tour of London'. Some creatures did live to venerable old age: the first grizzly bear seen in England, called Martin, was presented to George III by the Hudson Bay Company in 1811, and lived for 20 years.

Initially, the stock of lions relied on repeated gifts from other rulers to keep the numbers up, but finally the Tower succeeded in breeding its own. In June 1670, the youngest royal lion was given as a gift to the ruler of Denmark. Presumably, numbers were increasing faster than the older lions were dying off. By the end of the 18th century it could be reported that 'so much knowledge has been acquired of the art of rearing them, that we may boast now of an uninterrupted succession of British lions'.

However, the environment at the Tower was not ideal. Historian John Strype, who detailed the collection in his edition of Stow's *Survey of London*, published in 1720, complained: 'The creatures have a rank smell, which hath so affected the air of the place (tho' there is a garden adjoining) that it hath much injured the health of the man that attends them, and so stuffed up his head, that it affects his speech. And yet their dens are cleansed every day; and they have fresh water set them day and night.'

Some animals were clearly not happy. Ned Ward, who wrote the scurrilous *London Spy*, describes the behaviour of a leopard which 'loves not to be looked at. For as the madman will be apt to salute you with a bowl of chamber-lie, so will the leopard, if you come near him, stare in your face and piss on you, his urine being as hot as aqua fortis, and stinks worse than a polecat's.' Ward's pungent description suggests he knew whereof he spoke.

Elephants were considered particularly wise and noble beasts, and any ruler who couldn't boast that his private zoo contained one was regarded as rather shabby. James I, however, had the distinction of being the only British monarch to own an inebriated elephant. The royal zookeepers, working on false information that elephants could not safely drink water from April to September, used to give the animal a gallon of wine every day over the warmer months. It comes as no surprise to learn that, unlike most of the animals in his collection, James I's elephant was not displayed to the public...

Another animal that seemed to get his own back on his captors was a baboon, mentioned in the 1753 *Guide to the Menagerie* who 'will heave any Thing that happens to be within his reach with such Force as to split Stools, Bowls or any such wooden Utensils in a hundred Pieces'. While being shipped to England he threw 'a Cannon shot of nine Pounds Weight' at an unwary boy-sailor and killed him.

THAT'S ENTERTAINMENT

Like the Crown Jewels, the Royal Menagerie attracted first royal and noble visitors, then well-to-do gentlemen taking a tour of England from all across Europe, until it had become a lucrative tourist attraction. Even the Civil War clearly did not prevent foreign dignitaries visiting London or the Tower.

In June 1704, according to the then current edition of Stow's *Survey of London*, the **Tower Menagerie** consisted of: **six** lions, **two** leopards or tigers [quite hard to see how the writer was confused on this point, since it would be hard to find two more distinctively pelted great cats], **three** eagles, **two** Swedish owls ['of 'great biggness' called Hopkins'], **two** cats of the mountains [possibly mountain lions, or pumas?] and **one** jackal. Two stuffed **lions** were also on display.

By 1822, it contained only a **grizzly bear**, an **elephant** and a handful of birds – and none of the lions for which it, and **England**, had become famous.

Sebastian Gawareki, tutor to Prince Jan Sobieski of Poland, visited in 1647 and was delighted by 'a pair of lions, kept separately, very big beasts… two tigers and two lynxes, an old one and a young one and an Indian cat from Virginia'.

To maintain its attraction (and income), the Menagerie depended on entertainment value and novelty. On 21 July 1612 a special patent awarded Ralph Gill and Michael and Thomas Heneage the exclusive right to display big cats in England: 'that none duringe their lives shall carrie or convey any lion, lyonesses or Leopard to be shewed for gaine'. Despite this award, several private menageries sprung up as competition for the collection at the Tower. In 1697, this rather strange official advertisement, issued by the Tower, suggests it was seeking to maintain its monopoly on displaying wild animals: 'All persons whom it may concern, are desired to take notice, That the Master-keeper of his Majesty's Lion-office, in the Tower of London, is informed, that several wild beasts, against his Majesty's prerogative – royal, and the prohibition given and published to the contrary, as in the following, – That no person whatsoever, (except Thomas Dymocke, and the keeper of his Majesty's Lions for the time being), do for the future carry abroad, or expose to publick view, for their own private gain, any lions, lionesses, leopards, or any other beasts which are feroe natura as they will answer the contrary at their peril.'

Under this warning, the advertisement goes on to mention some of the most exotic attractions with the merest whiff of carnival hucksterism. The hyena from Aleppo, for instance, is described as 'the beast never seen in England before; he

---

Names given to the royal animals, according
to a children's guidebook from 1741 – the person
in charge of naming seems to have run out of names
before he ran out of animals:
Marco the Lion, Phillis his mate, Nero their son,
Jenny and Nanny the spare lionesses, Will the Leopard,
Will the Tiger, Phillis his mate, Dick, their son.

---

has such great strength that he breaks the biggest of ox-bones, and eats them'.

One of the wonders of the Tower during the late-17th century was the lion which befriended a dog. Teodor Billewcz, a Polish nobleman, recorded in his memoirs that the lion 'which can tear all the living creatures asunder, even the biggest ones, never wants to eat the dog, even when hungry'.

The first guidebook to the Menagerie, published in 1741, was a brief affair, but the 1753 guide, filled with very accurate engravings, is a joy to browse. The rarest animal in the Menagerie at that time, according to this publication, was an ostrich, a gift from the Dey of Tunis. The Dey had helpfully sent a pair, but one had swallowed a nail which 'stopt its Passage' and killed it. Ostriches seem to have fared particularly badly, because popular wisdom gave them the power to digest iron, a 'vulgar error' according to the guide, which 'has been long since exploded'. Unfortunately, an ostrich will eat iron and many other dangerous things quite freely. Clearly not enough people read the guide because, in

1791, another Tower ostrich died after ingesting 80 nails, presumably thrown into its cage by experimental onlookers.

In 1729 it cost 3d (£1.51) to visit the Menagerie – this when the average wage was 4 to 5s (£24.20 to £30.26) for an 80-hour working week. By 1741, the fee had risen to 6d (£2.98), beyond the pocket of most, but those that could afford it regarded it as a must-see. By 1830 people were happy to pay 1s (£3.39) to view the animals, but there was a good reason for this – a man named Alfred Cops, under whose charge the Menagerie thrived.

UP CLOSE AND PERSONAL

Alfred Cops was appointed Keeper of the struggling Royal Menagerie in 1822. He persuaded his employers that the Menagerie could be a lucrative business in its own right, and that they should buy exotic species rather than just rely on gifts, as other zoos did. By 1828 he had built the collection up to such an extent that the Menagerie now housed 60 different species, with over 280 animals in total. There was a room that measured 40ft which housed birds and grass-eating animals, while reptiles had been introduced in The Serpents' Room.

Visitors were allowed to get close to the animals, in part because of the restricted space. If you got too close to one of the female leopards, she would seize anything in range. Her favourites were hats, parasols and muffs and tear them to pieces, but this seems to have been regarded as something of a sideshow. Zebras were ridden around the exercise yard among the spectators (and, it is said, fed beer) and lion cubs were allowed to wander free between people's feet.

One popular, but short-lived, attraction in the early-19th century was the School of Monkeys. Onlookers entered a small room and apes were gradually let in, so that visitors could interact with them face to face. Unfortunately, this approach resulted in a boy nearly having his leg torn off, so these meet-and-greet sessions were hastily cancelled.

The potential danger undoubtedly added to the thrill. *The Times* of 6 October 1826 described a mishap while Cops entertained the tourists feeding a bird to a constricting snake: 'The snake darted at the bird, missed it, but seized the keeper by the thumb, and was coiled around his arm and neck in a moment. Mr Cops, who was alone, did not lose his presence of mind, and immediately attempted to relieve himself from the powerful constrictor, by pulling at its head: but it had so knotted itself upon its own head, Mr Cops could not reach it, and had thrown himself upon the floor, in order to grapple with a better chance of success, when two other keepers coming in, they broke the teeth of the serpent, and with some difficulty relieved Mr Cops from the fate of Laocoon [a Trojan priest of Apollo who was killed, along with his two sons, by two sea serpents for having warned his people of the Trojan horse].'

Newspapers from the time are peppered with lurid accounts of animal attacks, including a report on 6 January 1830 about a leopard attack on Joseph Croney, employed to remove bones and waste from the exercise yard at the Menagerie. Fortunately for Croney, two under-keepers heard his screams as the leopard jumped on him, and managed to beat it insensible with a fowling piece. He was treated for bites and claw marks. He made a full recovery.

Despite such reports (or perhaps because of them) the visitors kept coming, and *The Times* was moved to eulogise the collection in 1827 as a symbol of British superiority: 'Few objects are calculated to throw a greater lustre on our national character, in an emulative point of view, than the splendid specimens of savage nature which the resources of Government have succeeded in collecting. Birds, beasts, reptiles, in endless variety, press on the spectator's view and lead him through the labyrinth of wonderment superior to any ever before exhibited.'

'The poor fellow [Croney], seeing the perilous situation
in which he was placed, made for the keeper's apartment,
but before he could stir many paces, the infuriated beast
sprang from his den towards him.'
The Times, 6 January 1830

In its final years at the Tower, the Menagerie
increased significantly, and in 1829 zoologist
Edward Turner Bennett catalogued over
160 animals, ranging from snakes and kangaroos to
examples of most of the big cats:

A barbary lioness · Two tigers · Three leopards
· A jaguar · A puma · An ocelot · A caracal
· Two cheetahs · A striped hyena · A hyena-god
· Three African bloodhounds · A pair of Javanese civets
· A grey ichneumon · A paradoxurus · A brown coat
· A pair of raccoons · An American black bear
· A grizzly bear · A Tibet bear · A Bornean bear ·
Monkeys · A bonnetted monkey · A pig-faced baboon
· A baboon · Two white-headed mongooses
· Three kangaroos · An African porcupine · An Asiatic elephant
· A zebra · Two llamas
· One Malaysian Eusa-deer
· An albino Indian antelope · An African sheep
· A great sea eagle · A golden eagle · A bearded Griffin
· A griffin vulture · A secretary bird
· A Virginian horned owl · A deep-blue Macaw
· A blue and yellow Macaw
· A yellow crested cockatoo
· Two emus · A crowned crane
· A pair of pelicans from Hungary
· An alligator · An Indian boa
· Two anacondas
· 100 rattlesnakes, varying in length from 4ft to 6ft

A combination of visitor pressure, number of animals and a lack of facilities led to the eventual dissolution of the Royal Menagerie. When, in August 1830, 150 of the Menagerie's animals were presented to the newly formed Zoological Society of London, it was the beginning of the end. However, the society drained land and built enclosures for their animals in Regent's Park, and London Zoo came into being.

For a while Alfred Cops was allowed to keep on at the Tower the animals he had himself purchased and charge 6d (£1.70), half the previous rate, to see them. Cops's great problem, both before and after the reduction of the animal numbers, seems to have been safety. Even with a much-reduced roll-call, accidents still happened with disturbing regularity. In April 1834, a wolf escaped. One suspects that people were looking for a way to get rid of Cops and his odiferous private enterprise scheme, and now the Menagerie was no longer official, it was on borrowed time. The Constable of the Tower at this time was the Duke of Wellington, who by happy chance was also one of the founder members of the Zoological Society. (Not often thought of as an animal lover, Wellington was consulted in 1828 on the most suitable way of keeping a giraffe when the first one was bought to London, and was well placed to keep the peace between the various departments within the Tower while considering a better environment for the animals.) Discussions between the Duke and William IV (1830-1837) concluded: 'The King is determined that the Wild Beasts shall not be kept there.'

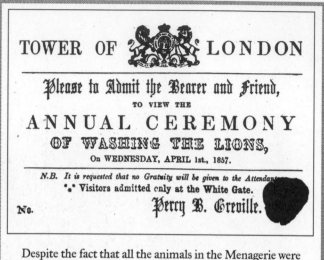

TOWER OF 🦁 LONDON

Please to Admit the Bearer and Friend,

TO VIEW THE

ANNUAL CEREMONY

OF WASHING THE LIONS,

On WEDNESDAY, APRIL 1st., 1857.

N.B. It is requested that no Gratuity will be given to the Attendants.

*** Visitors admitted only at the White Gate.

No.   **Percy B. Greville.**

Despite the fact that all the animals in the Menagerie were given to the nascent Royal Zoological Society in the 1830s, for several decades afterwards **practical jokers** would periodically place adverts in the newspapers announcing that the **lions would be publicly washed** at the Tower on 1 April. The gullible would buy fake tickets and arrive in their thousands, blocking the surrounding streets.

The Menagerie finally officially closed on 28 August 1835 (shortly after one Ensign Seymour got his leg bitten by a monkey, which may have been the last straw). The remaining animals were sold to American showman, Benjamin Franklin Brown, who would go on to marry Cops's daughter in 1841. Cops remained in the Keeper's House until his death in 1853, living just long enough to see the Lion Tower and Menagerie demolished, and a new ticket office built in their place.

CHAPTER

✠

MAKING A MINT

✠

or Mr Finch, Moneyer at the Tower's Mint, the morning of 20 December 1798 began like any other: supervising guardsmen operating the coin presses and checking each freshly minted coin before locking it in a chest. But when he sent the men to breakfast at 9 o'clock, 28-year-old James Turnbull and another returned almost immediately. Turnbull pulled out a gun and demanded the keys to the money chest. (According to some accounts the second soldier, Dalton, was his accomplice and kept watch, but Turnbull later attempted to clear him, testifying: 'He knew nothing at all about this… he ran away and gave an alarm to the serjeant of the guard.'). Neither an elderly witness's outburst: 'Are you mad, are you in your senses?', nor Finch's attempt to wrest the gun from him stopped Turnbull from opening the chest and making away with four bags of guineas.

Turnbull never had time to enjoy his newly minted wealth, though. He was apprehended at Dover attempting to leave the country with over 1,000 guineas on his person. On 20 February 1799 he was found guilty of theft with violence at the Old Bailey and sentenced to death. In keeping with the Mint's reputation for exactness, 8d (£2.10 in modern terms) was added to his total haul in respect of the bags he used to carry it off in.

The first Mint didn't move into the Tower precincts until the reign of Edward I, when it was still one of only several mints in the country. However, from 1553, the Tower Mint became the sole place that English coinage could be struck, and it remained so until the recoinage crisis of the 1690s.

COINS OF THE REALM

By the time of Turnbull's audacious robbery, the Royal Mint at the Tower had been producing coins of the realm for more than 500 years. Initially just one of several places where coins were struck, the Royal Mint at the Tower eventually became the major, and at one point, the only, centre of coin making in the country.

There is evidence of money being struck by a number of small workshops in London since Anglo-Saxon times, the earliest record being from 825. By the time William I conquered England there was already the beginnings of a unified English currency, introduced by King Edgar (959-975), a silver penny of standard weight and design produced by many small mints across the country. Historically, since England had been a series of kingdoms ruled by oft-warring tribes of different ethnic backgrounds and had their own monetary systems, this level of financial standardisation was quite an achievement. William the Conqueror was able to build on this sound base, and for the next two centuries English currency was relatively stable. It is around this time that foreign documents begin to refer to the coins as 'sterling pennies'.

In the Middle Ages, inflation was very low and values of coins didn't change much, but there was a constant need to replenish stock for another, very practical reason. Nowadays, we are so used to monetary value being represented in other forms – notes, credit cards and electronic transfers – that we find it hard to comprehend what it was like to live in a world where the value of a coin related directly to the metal out of which it was made. Coins were often cut up into smaller pieces to give change – a halfpenny was exactly that: a penny cut in half. A nefarious but widespread act was shaving or clipping small amounts of the metal off a coin, physically cheating the owner of its worth.

> **Counterfeiting coins** was a heinous crime that carried heavy penalties. Anyone caught doing so would be punished by having their **right hand cut off**, and being castrated.

The mints had a very good idea of what was happening to coinage because, while new coins went out, old ones returned in the form of taxes collected around the country. Edward I began to issue a new coinage because of wear and clipping, and in a bid to make any unlawful shaving more evident, the cross on one side of the coins was extended to its very edges. He also set about building a new, bigger Mint at the Tower – in 1300 the Mint building is described as being 400ft long – which was increasingly the main source of coinage. Bringing the various workshops into one enclave helped with standardisation and efficiency, although there remained other mints throughout the country, including a well-known one at Canterbury.

Early in the reign of Richard II money began to be devalued, and clipping became so extensive that it is reckoned up to 20% of the silver in circulation was stolen this way, which must have left some very odd-shaped coins. To add to the problems, the majority of English currency was being sent abroad, which led to a shortage of small denomination coins. This made it extremely difficult for the poor – the majority of his citizens – to carry out day-to-day transactions. Parliament recorded that the Mint would remedy the lack of small change as soon as the king provided bullion for them to melt down and make coins, but this did not seem to be forthcoming. In fact, it wasn't until Henry Tudor, having seized the throne in 1485, found his money 'sore ympeyred as well by clippyng therof as counterfettyng of the same' that a solution to the problem – milling the edges of the coins – was first tried.

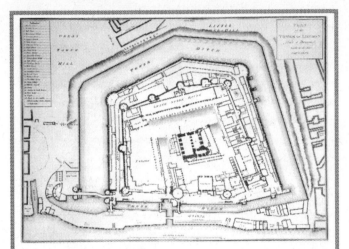

By **1423** there were **four** major mints in operation: The Tower, Calais [officially part of England until **1558**], York and Bristol. All were under the charge of the same Master, at that time **Bartholomew Goldbeter**, clearly named for his family's involvement in the gold trade. Calais was by far the most productive, striking on average nearly six times as many coins as the **Tower Mint**.

According to the **Pipe Rolls of the Exchequer** of Edward I, in 1275-1285 £729.17s.8 1/2d [**£289,000**] was spent on building and equipment for the Mint, and refers to 'the little tower where the treasure of the mint is kept', probably in the region of Mint Street. This was an extraordinary sum at a time when it is estimated that there was approximately **£20,000** [**£7 million**] in circulation in the entire country.

When Henry VIII split with the Roman Catholic church in the following century, he seized the riches of its many monasteries and churches within his kingdom, and the Mint became a hive of activity, smelting down and turning the purloined riches into cash. People worked day and night to deal with vast amounts of precious metal, producing the coinage demanded by a cash-strapped Treasury. Such was the pressure on the Mint that for a short time a second mint was opened in Southwark, across the river from the Tower.

Despite all of this, by the end of his reign Henry VIII had undone much of his father's work of safeguarding the value of the kingdom's coinage. It wasn't until Elizabeth I addressed the problem that English money would regain its reputation. The historian Holinshed connected her reform of the coinage with her reform of the Church, noting she achieved 'a certeine perfection, purenesse, and soundness, as here in hir new stamps and coines of all sorts; so also in God's religion, setting the material churches of hir dominions free from all popish trash'.

As a monarch, your spending power ultimately depended on the gold and silver you could lay your hands on. If you needed more it usually meant sending expeditions off to find it in foreign lands, as the Spanish did in Mexico, or to steal it from someone else, as the English frequently did on the Spanish Main. If supplies from mines and plunder were insufficient, you could deflate the value of coins by introducing other, less expensive metals, as Henry VIII did in the latter years of his reign. If you did this, though, you then had to recall and remake all the coins at the new value.

The Tower Mint was kept feverishly active throughout the 16th century, first with processing Henry VIII's 'acquisitions' from the dissolution of the monasteries and his devaluation of the coinage, and later on behalf of his daughters when they came to the throne. In 1554 the Mint was presented with 20 cartloads of silver, worth £17,600 (around £3.8 million in modern terms), as part of Mary I's marriage contract with Philip of Spain. This Spanish silver – all 97 chests of it – had to be smelted and re-minted. Then the coinage was devalued and re-minted again in Elizabeth I's reign. As a result of all this work, more space was created for the Mint between 1560 and 1562 in the form of a new building erected near the Salt Tower, in the southern part of the Outer Ward: the typical Tudor brick and timber framework building in the Outer Ward which became known as the Upper Mint. Additionally, a new refining house, where gold and silver were melted, impurities removed

During one particularly busy period in 1546, the maker of melting pots at the Southwark Mint, William Foxley, fell asleep for 14 days and 15 nights, waking 'as if he had slept but one'. He continued to make melting pots in the Tower until his death in 1587.

and other metals added, was constructed to the south of the White Tower. The 18th-century Mint Administrative Offices, just to the north of the Byward Tower, is thought to stand on the site of an earlier administrative centre which, by 1585/86, was needed to keep track of operations in the many separate Mint buildings contained within the Tower's precincts.

By the mid-17th century the stability of English coinage was again threatened by increasing amounts of clipping, shaving and grinding – so rife was this practice that some wags reckoned it was harder to find an unshaved coin than a shaved one. In 1669 huge amounts of money were recalled and recoined, incorporating a milled edge which would, it was hoped, make any tampering immediately evident. To accommodate all this extra work the Mint took over yet more of the Outer Ward, ejecting the garrison from two buildings and leading the Lieutenant of the Tower to complain that his men were forced to sleep three to a bed, so cramped were their remaining quarters. But the Mint continued to expand. Sir Christopher Wren was already occupied with building more accommodation, in addition to several different workshops that were being erected in the garden of the Mint Comptroller's house, situated between the Broad Arrow Tower and the Constable Tower.

Since the 16th century, much of the area between the inner and outer walls had been known as The Mint, and by the beginning of the 18th century occupied every inch of the Outer Ward, wrapping around the west, north and east sides of the walls, with the Irish Mint tucked in the south-east corner, and buildings crammed in on both sides, making the road running down the middle very narrow in places.

> **'Great contentions** do daily arise among the King's
> Subjects in Fairs, Markets, Shops. Persons, before they
> conclude in any Bargains, are necessitated first to settle the
> Price of the Value of the very Money they are to Receive for
> their Goods; and if it be in Guineas at a High Rate or in Bad
> Moneys they set the Price of their Goods accordingly.'
> *Report of the Treasury Secretary in the 1690s on the problems*
> *caused by the excessive amount of forged and debased coinage*

By then the Mint consisted of numerous departments, including separate gold and silver smelting houses and the Assay Office, where the metal was tested, was tucked between them on the west side. The houses of various officials such as the Master of the Mint and Warden and Deputy Warden were to the north, while a mixture of functions were taken care of in the eastern part, including the stables, the washhouse and the refinery workshops.

CAREERS WITH COINS

The Mint always stood apart from the rest of life within the Tower. Indeed, until 1688 it was an entirely independent body complete with its own rather arcane hierarchy. While otherwise keeping themselves to themselves in their special enclosure, its employees would still contribute to certain activities within the Tower while completely ignoring others. One of their particular interests was the upkeep of the Chapel Royal of St Peter ad Vincula, to which they continued to contribute even after the Mint had been removed from the Tower.

From the time of Edward I, the ultimate power within the confines of the Mint was its Master. Despite the key part the Mint played in the control of the country's power and wealth, some Masters, such as Nicholas Malakin, were foreigners. Malakin, who was in charge during the latter years of the reign of Richard II, came from Florence, where Europe's canniest bankers, such as the Medici family, were soon to flourish.

The Master of the Mint reported to the King's Treasurer and was assisted by a Warden, a Comptroller and an Assay Master. During the 13th and 14th centuries, Officers at the Tower Mint often held the same position for other mints, such as the one in Calais, which used dies created at the Tower.

The dies, worked by skilled engravers, were a precious commodity, for if they were substandard or, worse, fell into the wrong hands, they could be a serious threat to the stability of the currency. The engraver was answerable to the Clerk of the Irons for any worn or faulty dies. These had to be handed over to him for disposal on a monthly basis, and were then

---

'As the Moroccan sequins were of superior quality, the royal mint in the Tower of London seized the opportunity to remelt them, debasing them with an English copper alloy. The official debasement of the coinage, begun in the 1540s, was called in numismatic parlance 'la mutacion du poids' and 'la mutacion de la matiere.' In consequence of this mutation, the English angel [...] was, numismatically, a coin of bastard quality, a cross-breed.'
Gustav Ungerer, 'Portia and the Prince of Morocco', *Shakespeare Studies, Vol* 31

In addition to the **Master** and the **Assay Master** [whose
job it was to measure and record the bullion brought in to the
Mint, and without whose seal no coins could be released into
circulation] there were many interesting-sounding posts attached
to the Mint, but most now sadly lost. There was a Surveyor of the
Meltings, a Clerk of the Irons, and the grand-sounding
Provost of the Company of Moneyers. The Company of
Moneyers, which once took care of the physical manufacture of
the coins, ceased to exist in the 19th century. One unusual early
post was that of the **Cuneator**, who was responsible for the
engravers who created the dies from which coins were struck
[*cuneus* is the Latin for 'die']. It was a hereditary position until
Richard II decided to appoint his own engravers.

thoroughly defaced in the presence of the Warden, Comptroller
and Master of the Mint. Perfectly engraved dies, however,
became the responsibility of the Keeper of the Irons, who
was charged with tracking what happened to them.

The duties of the Master were at times split between a
Commission, as it was just before the Civil War, when both Sir
Ralph Freeman and Sir Thomas Aylesbury were responsible for
the Mint, or during the financial uncertainties of the 1680s,
when two trios of commissioners were employed to keep the
coinage stable. One, Sir Henry Slingsby, was suspended in 1680
for falling behind in his account keeping, although he did not
resign until 1685. It was Slingsby who proposed what became
known as the 'standard solution'. This sought to balance free
market trading with a series of rules that aimed to maintain

coin value and keep currency in circulation. Gold coins had their own intrinsic value. Rather than just being symbols of buying power, people tended to hoard them, so naturally, this resulted in shortages.

In 1688 the Treasury took over control of the Mint, although the Tower's Master of the Mint still remained a powerful and responsible figure. One of the most famous Masters of the Mint was Sir Isaac Newton, who was appointed in 1699 and held the post for 28 years. For the previous three years he had been Warden of the Mint and was responsible for the success of the extensive recoinage after devaluation in 1696. No doubt he ensured the latest technology was employed, as he needed every new development available not just to improve efficiency, but to proof the coinage from counterfeiters and shavers.

Newton was used to an academic life, but he adapted to business very quickly. His first move was to analyse the manufacturing process in what we would now call a time and motion study, so as to better understand and improve it. Thanks to his observations he speeded up the line of production to such an extent that instead of the 25 coins a minute – which was

'Two mills with four millers, 12 horses, two horse keepers, three cutters, two flatters, eight sizers, one nealer, three blanchers, two markers, two presses with 14 labourers to pull at them can coin after the rate of a thousand weight or 3,000 lib [pounds] of money per diem.'

Sir Isaac Newton's calculation for the productivity of the Royal Mint in 1699.

considered extremely efficient in the 17th century – the Mint increased manufacture to between 50 and 55 coins a minute. Newton also spent a great deal of energy protecting the space given over to the Mint from the encroachment of the two other powerful figures within the Tower's rather uncertain hierarchy: the Lieutenant of the Tower and the Master of the Ordnance. All three continually jockeyed for position and power.

As Master of the Mint, Sir Isaac was expected to look into various matters relating to fiscal topics, as well as ensuring the smooth running of all the various Mint departments. He produced a whole range of Mint Reports for the Treasury that

DIES.

the Coining press in the Tower.

Despite the fact he was 57 when appointed Master of the Royal Mint, Sir Isaac Newton was so excited by his role that he used to arrive at the Tower of London at 4 o'clock in the morning to watch the first pressing of coins.

give us a good idea of the breadth of the Mint's involvement and the extent of the Master's duties and influence. These duties ranged from answers to queries from the Treasury about the value of various foreign currencies (such as on Sweden's Rix dollars, German Reichsthaler and Lübische Mark) and assessments of the strength of other currencies (for example, the report 'On the Proportion of Gold and Silver in Value in several European currencies') to evaluations of various schemes and trials (Memorial about Tryall of the Copper Coynage, Ireland).

Until 1699 the Master was appointed for life, and might also hold other offices within the Tower, or in later years within the government. The post was finally abolished in 1870, and the running of the Mint became part of the responsibility of the Chancellor of the Exchequer's Office. To this day, however, the Chancellor also holds the honorary title Master of the Mint.

MAKING MONEY

We know little about how the Mint operated through the Middle Ages. Excavations around Legge's Mount have revealed some tantalising glimpses of activity from the 15th century, including several large and small metal working vessels, but very little other evidence remains.

For most of their history, coins have been struck – that is, a hand-made disc of softish metal is put between two moulds, and with one swift blow from a hammer the design on the moulds is simultaneously imprinted on both sides of the coin. This method, which was first recorded in the Iron Age, continued to be employed, fundamentally unchanged, for centuries, and we know from early wages records that the Master of the Mint employed skilled craftsmen to process and refine metals and strike them into hand-stamped coins.

The first machinery introduced to the Mint was in 1554, and it is thought to be similar to the presses known to have been installed at the Paris Mint in 1552. More complex mechanical presses were starting to be introduced across Europe in the late-16th century. Screw-operated devices speeded up the coining process, and these became standard in the Mint from around 1662. Although these machines still worked on single coins, they allowed 20 (or even 25) coins a minute to be produced – provided the workmen slipping the blanks into place were deft enough. It was said you could spot employees of the Mint by the number of finger ends they were missing. Rolling machines that flattened the softened metal to the required thickness before blanks were cut out of it were also introduced.

Even with mechanical presses, minting coins was still a labour-intensive process. Striking the coins still needed a relay of men to feed the press, as well as skilled craftsmen to process the metals, which went through several different workshops before they were ready to be struck. Silver is too soft to make durable coins out of without it being mixed with a hardening agent such as copper – copper was desirable because it didn't alter the colour of silver. After it was purified, the metal passed through another workshop for annealing, where the metal was beaten out in an even sheet which was designed to reorder its atomic structure and make it ready to take a clean impression.

In order to support **the Cornish tin-mining industry**, Queen Anne compelled the Royal Mint to buy at least 1,600 tons of tin at £70 [£7,559] a ton, and it struggled to fulfil the function of an impromptu 'Tin Marketing Board' until this rather strange duty was handed off to the Prince of Wales, whose Duchy it affected the most.

Then the silver would be checked for quality, to make sure an unscrupulous silversmith hadn't added too much copper, before moving to another workshop where it was cleaned with acid, known as blanching. And so precious metal progressed from one building to another, being rolled into sheets, cut into pieces, stamped, recorded, vouched for and finally dispatched.

The Byward Tower is thought to have been occupied by someone in charge of the Royal Mint during Richard II's reign. Although damaged now, its wall paintings include an archangel weighing souls at the Last Judgement, which would have been considered a suitable subject for an apartment occupied by such a dignitary [and perhaps a quiet reminder of his duty].

Visiting the Mint had always been a fashionable pastime, particularly among scientifically inclined young men. Peter Cunningham's *Handbook of London*, from 1850, describes how a visit might be arranged. First you had to obtain an Order from the Master of the Mint 'available only for the day specified', on which 'the names and addresses of the persons wishing to be admitted, or of some one of them, with the number of the rest, are to be stated. The person or persons named in the application are held responsible for those accompanying them'. In describing what the visitor can expect to see, Cunningham's guide sums up the complexities involved in coin manufacture: 'The various processes connected with coining are carried on by a series of ingenious machines in certain rooms known as the rolling room, the cutting-out room, the milling room, the analysing room, the coining press room, etc. The most curious process is that called the drawing-bench, by which the metal, when tested to show that it contains the proper alloy, is drawn through rollers to the precise thickness required for the coin which is to be cut out of it. In the case of gold, the difference of a hair's breadth in any part of the plate or sheet of gold would alter the value of a sovereign. By another machine, circular disks are punched out of the sheets of metal of any size required, and by a number of screw presses these blanks, as they are called, are stamped on observe and reverse at the same time. The force with which the blow is struck; the rapid motion by which 60 or 70 sixpences may be struck in a minute, and half-crowns or sovereigns in minor proportions; the mode in which the press feeds itself with the blanks to be coined, and, when struck, removes them from between the dies, is very interesting. The mode of forming the dies, and the hardening of them by a chemical process, are kept secret.'

Ever since the 13th century, coins produced by the Mint have been assayed, to ensure that they came up to standard. It was the Master of the Mint who had the final word on standards throughout the year, and penalties for unacceptable quality, either in the metal or the craftsmanship, fell on him, because it was essential the Master did his job well and

In 1489, under **Henry VII**, the largest gold coin struck in England at the time was minted at the Tower. It was four centimetres round and weighed 15.5g. On one side was an image of the king on his throne holding the **Orb and Sceptre,** which is what gave rise to the name 'sovereign' as the coin's name.

honestly. It was the Master who would have to make good any shortfall if coins were produced just slightly under weight when coins were tested each year at the Trial of the Pyx.

MOVING THE MINT

Eventually the Mint had to be removed from the Tower because there was no more room left. It had already squeezed several other offices out, and its production capacity was being severely limited by lack of space. Finally, in 1798 the Privy Council took the decision to rehouse the whole Mint. The New Mint didn't go far; a bespoke home for all the various processes, hidden behind a fashionable Palladian facade designed by James Johnson and Robert Smirke, was built on a mound called Little Tower Hill to the north-east of the Tower. The Mint moved to its new location in 1810 and coin production continued up until 1978, when the whole facility was moved to Llantrisant, in South Wales, providing a huge saving, but bringing to an end a rather grand tradition.

There used to be dozens of different mints creating coinage around the country, but only one, apart from the Royal Mint, still survives: The Birmingham Mint. The Birmingham Mint produces millions of euros and other coins for other countries, as well as vending tokens and commemorative medals. The first contract to produce another country's coinage was undertaken in the early 1550s, during Mary I's reign, when the Mint made coins for Spain.

CHAPTER

✠

CROWN JEWELS

✠

ne of the most commonly asked questions by people facing the priceless splendour of the Crown Jewels is: 'Are they real?'. The answer, most emphatically, is yes. The gem-encircled golden Orb has been placed in the hand of the monarch at every coronation since 1661, and the sapphire and ruby coronation ring is the one made for William IV. Some of the world's largest and most famous gems are here, including the enormous pear-shaped diamond in the Sovereign's Sceptre with Cross. The Sceptre is the symbol of the monarch's temporal power, and contains the First Star of Africa (more prosaically known as Cullinan I), the largest top-quality cut diamond in the world.

The collection in the Jewel House is a varied ensemble, not only including the coronation regalia but also banqueting plate, church plate, the coronation robes, woven in gold thread, and christening fonts still used by the Royal Family.

The Imperial State Crown, mounted with more than 3,000 precious jewels, is perhaps the most famous and most recognisable crown on display. This is the crown that Queen

---

The Cullinan Diamond, **the biggest diamond ever found** [weighing 3,106 carats] was discovered near Pretoria in 1905, and named after the mining company's chairman, Sir Thomas Cullinan. The Transvaal government bought it for £150,000 as a birthday gift for King Edward VII. The uncut diamond was sent to Europe anonymously by parcel post while a decoy package was sent on a heavily guarded ship. The outsize rock was cut into nine major and 96 minor diamonds, in a cutting process that took around **eight months**.

George IV [1820-1830], better known to most people as the **fun-loving and spendthrift Prince Regent,** had an extraordinarily sumptuous crown made up for his coronation in 1831. It required **12,314 diamonds,** far more than the state could muster, so 'Prinny' hired the necessary gemstones from the Crown Jewellers, Rundell, Bridge and Rundell, fully expecting Parliament to vote him the money to buy them outright. This the Commons steadfastly refused to do – he'd been a prodigiously expensive prince – and after two years of arguing, the stones were finally returned.

Elizabeth II wears during the State Opening of Parliament each year. It was made for George VI's coronation in 1937, but contains many of the stones set in its precursors from the 17th, 18th and 19th centuries.

The great sapphire set in the Maltese cross at the top of this crown comes, according to legend, from a ring worn by Edward the Confessor and retrieved when his body was moved to Westminster Abbey in 1163. The Stuart Sapphire at the back of the crown is almost as old, believed to have been set in the crown of Alexander II of Scotland in 1214. It was taken to England along with the symbolic Stone of Scone, but a peripatetic existence sent it into the hands of the founder of the Stuarts, then back and forth among generations of English and Scottish royal families. It was set in the Imperial State Crown in 1838 but moved from the front to the back to accommodate the Second Star of Africa (Cullinan II), which now sits below the Black Prince's Ruby. This large ruby (technically a spinel, not a true ruby) was a gift, it was said, in recognition of the shelter from battle the Black Prince gave to the king of Castile, Pedro El Cruel, in 1367. It has always been considered a lucky stone, and Henry V carried it in his helmet at Agincourt.

The worth of the Crown Jewels, measured in gold and gems, is staggering, but there is a symbolic and historic value to the coronation regalia in particular that is beyond price.

A HISTORICAL SYMBOL

On 22 April 1661, the day before St George's Day, Londoners crowded the streets to cheer Charles II's resplendent progress as he made his way from the Tower to Westminster to prepare for his coronation. After 12 years of sombre piety under the Protectorate and Parliamentary rule, the sight of the restored king in his bejewelled robes must have stirred the hearts of those lucky enough to find a place to watch. One of them was Samuel Pepys, who wrote in his diary: 'I can say that besides the pleasure of the sight of these glorious things, I may now shut my eyes against any other objects, or for the future trouble myself to see things of state and shewe, as being sure never to see the like again in this world.'

When Charles I left London to begin fighting the Civil War, he left behind the majority of the royal jewels at the Tower, in the charge of Sir Henry Mildmay. Mildmay, however, quickly declared for parliament, against the Crown. King Charles appointed a new Master of the Jewel House, but since most of the jewels were in Mildmay's care, this was a futile gesture.

At this time the coronation regalia was still held at Westminster Abbey. To ensure that it hadn't been smuggled out

Queen Elizabeth The Queen Mother's crown is set with the famous Indian diamond, the Koh-i-Noor, which translates as 'Mountain of Light'. The diamond is said to bring bad luck to any male wearer. Since its arrival in Britain in 1850, it has only been worn by women.

to the king, parliament ordered the 'Locks of the Doors where the Regalia are kept in Westminster Abbey' to be opened on 3 June 1643, and Mildmay and Henry Marten, an MP, to draw up a careful list of everything present, and then change the locks. Peter Heylyn, Treasurer of the Chapter of Westminster and Charles I's former chaplain, described Marten's derision of the royal jewels: '[taking out] the Crowns, the Robes, the Swords, and Scepter, belonging anciently to K Edward the Confessor, and used by all our Kings at their Inaugurations with a scorn greater than his Lusts and the rest of His vices, he openly declares, That there would be no further use of those Toyes and Trifles And in the jollity of that humour, invests George Withers [another member of the party] in the Royall Habiliments Who being thus Crownd and arrayd (as right well became him) first marcht about the Room with a stately Garb and afterwards with a thousand Apish and Ridiculous actions exposed those sacred ornaments to contempt and laughter.'

After two years of hard (and expensive) fighting, the House of Commons debated that the royal plate be melted down and turned into coinage to fund the parliamentarian cause. The Lords' argument that it 'is ancient Plate; the Fashion of it, and the Badges upon it, were worth more than the Plate itself' was overruled. As well as the coronation regalia, the treasures included hundreds of gold and silver items, including banqueting plate and coronets, and they were expected to yield about £3,000 (around £387,621 in modern terms) in coins. On 16 November 1644 Sir Henry Mildmay handed it over to the Mint for smelting down and minting.

Perhaps because they were afraid of public outcry or of rallying monarchist sympathisers, Parliament did nothing to the coronation regalia itself until the Civil War was over. But in July 1649, six months after Charles I's head had rolled off the block, the Government passed a bill to sell off the personal estate of the royal family and 'cause the same [the Crown Jewels] to be totally broken', the gold and silver melted down and the individual jewels sold off. Since the Crown Jewels held a historic and spiritual significance way beyond their intrinsic value, with this act the Commonwealth was striking at the heart of the idea that kings ruled by divine right. Much of the coronation regalia dated back more than six centuries, including the crown of the saintly Edward the Confessor, with which English monarchs had ever since been crowned. After Edward's canonisation in 1161, the kings and queens of England had been carrying and wearing not just ancient symbols of the longevity of monarchy, but holy relics. Getting rid of the regalia was a powerful symbol of the new world order: 'Now Edwards Staffe is broken, Chair overturned, Cloaths rent, and Crown melted; our present Age esteeming them the Reliques of Superstition.'

Sir Henry Mildmay was once again called upon to make an inventory, assisted by his cousin, Carew Hervey Mildmay, and to hand over responsibility to the trustees in charge of the sale of the former king's possessions. However, Carew Mildmay

When Mary II [1689-1694], was crowned alongside her husband, William III [1689-1702], a second set of coronation regalia was required because they were joint monarchs. The Orb created for Mary was only ever used on this one occasion; it was set with hired stones and later set with imitation stones, **some of which are more than 300 years old.**

suffered a sudden change of heart, locked himself in the Jewel House and refused the trustees admittance for over six weeks. Finally they lost patience and had the building stormed. Carew Mildmay was thrown in the Fleet prison.

The Imperial State Crown was reckoned to be worth £1,100 (about £92,000 in modern terms) in gold and gems but St Edward's Crown, probably because of the quality of the gold, was only worth £248 (about £21,000 in modern terms), and the queen's coronation crown was valued at a mere £16 (about £13,000 in modern terms). Almost everything was sold, including broken storage chests and the carpet from the floor of the old Jewel House. They also sold off some of the more novel items in the collection, such as several 'unicorn horns', valued at £600 (about £50,000 in modern terms). Only a tiny number of items escaped the cull, including a gold and silver-covered Bible and Book of Common Prayer.

When Charles II was restored to the throne in 1660 there was a rush to get ready for his coronation. Sir Henry Mildmay, summoned to account for the Crown Jewels left in his keeping, tried to flee, but was caught at Rye, on the Kent coast; he was sentenced to be dragged through the streets every year on the anniversary of Charles I's death.

It rapidly became clear to the Privy Council, in charge of organising the coronation, that nothing remained with which to crown the king. Undaunted, they commissioned replicas of the old Crown Jewels – fortunately they had the inventory made by the Parliamentarians. The cost of the new coronation regalia, made by goldsmith Robert Vyner, was around £15,000 (about £1.6 million in modern terms), over half of it accounted for by the new coronation crown.

THE ROYAL CROWNS

Although St Edward's is the symbolic crown of the sovereign, many monarchs and their consorts have had their own personal crowns made. Queen Victoria's Small Diamond Crown is tiny, weighing just 6oz and is covered with 1,187 diamonds. The Imperial Crown of India, set with 6,002 diamonds, was made for George V to wear at the Delhi Durbar in 1911. The English coronation regalia could not legally be taken out of the country, so this crown was specially made for the event. It has only been worn once.

Although there are few early records, it seems likely that, as one of the strongest fortresses in the land, the Tower of London would have been a home for at least some of the monarch's treasures from the moment it was built. There is a vault in the basement of the White Tower, built at the foot of a corner

> The Imperial State Crown is set with 2,868 diamonds,
> 17 sapphires, 11 emeralds, 5 rubies and 273 pearls.
> ### It weighs 1,006kg

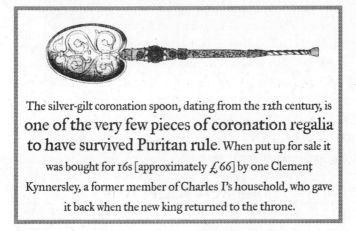

The silver-gilt coronation spoon, dating from the 12th century, is **one of the very few pieces of coronation regalia to have survived Puritan rule**. When put up for sale it was bought for 16s [approximately £66] by one Clement Kynnersley, a former member of Charles I's household, who gave it back when the new king returned to the throne.

buttress, where the structural strength of the building was at its greatest, which is thought to be where William the Conqueror kept his treasure. In the sub-crypt beneath the Chapel Royal of St John the Evangelist there is a small cell where ornaments, particularly those in frequent use for services, were kept.

The first actual mention we have of what might be considered the Crown Jewels comes in the reign of Edward II, when an inventory of the king's possessions lists gold plate, jewels and coronets together. At the time they were the personal possession of the ruler, and sometimes wound up 'in hock' to allow the king to pay for costly activities such as building new fortifications or going on crusade.

The royal household developed a section dealing specifically with the sovereign's jewels, plate and precious metal objects in the early 15th century, when the functions of the Jewel House were divided from those of the Great Wardrobe. The Master of the Jewel House, along with his

The Sovereign's Orb and Sceptre, made
for the coronation of Charles II in 1660, have been used
at every subsequent coronation, including that of
Queen Elizabeth II in 1953.

Clerk, Yeoman and Groom, were responsible for the care and
security of all items made of precious metals, whether they
had jewels set in them or not, and were answerable to the
monarch. They had offices in other royal palaces, but most of
these precious items were kept at the Tower and sent out to
other residences when required for particular functions.

A map of the Tower of London, drawn by William Haiward
and John Gascoyne in 1597, shows a two-storey building

against the south wall of the White Tower labelled 'Jewel House', which had been rebuilt thanks to Thomas Cromwell, Earl of Essex, in his role as Master of the Jewel House (1532-1540). The original building on that spot, built in 1508, was a thick-walled strong room containing chests full of plate and what were described as cases for the jewels. There was also a room in another building nearby for counting and weighing (presumably to ensure no one had clipped a bit of gold off the edge of one of the vessels during a state banquet) as well as a library for record keeping and a privy. The Jewel House was chiefly concerned with supplying the vast amounts of gold and silver objects for official banquets and receptions. The collection in the Tower did, however, include all the extra crowns and regalia used on other state occasions.

The strong room beside the White Tower seems to have been put back to its old usage to house Charles II's royal regalia, and for the first time everything was kept together. In 1666, the Great Fire of London demonstrated how open to threat the White Tower was if another fire broke out, especially since the White Tower at the time contained large stores of gunpowder. Following the Great Fire, the Crown Jewels were rehoused in the ground floor of the Martin Tower, probably during 1669.

STOP THIEF!

It was shortly after their removal to the Martin Tower that one of the most infamous episodes in the history of the Crown Jewels took place: the attempt to steal them by Colonel Blood.

The Master of the Jewel House at this time was Sir Gilbert Talbot. Like many during this period, Master of the Jewel House was in a number of ways an honorary title, and Talbot employed an old retainer, Talbot Edwards, to act as a live-in keeper, rather than occupy the Master's quarters in the Martin Tower himself. Edwards made a living collecting small sums from visitors wishing to view the royal treasure. (Sir Gilbert Talbot had complained that the salary for his appointment was so low that he could not afford to pay Edwards, but he received tacit consent from the king for Edwards to 'show the regalia to strangers' and keep any tips they might give him. He must have received quite a few, because Sir Gilbert was offered 500 pieces of gold from someone who wanted the post after Edwards died in 1674.)

In the early months of 1671 an elderly clergyman and his wife (actually the wily adventurer Thomas Blood in disguise, with an

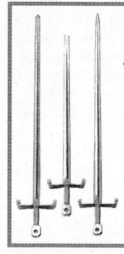

The three Swords of Justice all date from around 1626. The Sword of Spiritual Justice and the Sword of Temporal Justice are sharp, but the Sword of Mercy, known as 'Curtana', has a blunt end, in keeping with the tradition of mercy. The earliest mention of the presence of swords among the Crown Jewels dates to the coronation of Richard I in 1189, when swords were carried in his coronation procession, possibly representing his triple kingdoms of England, Normandy and Anjou.

accomplice) visited the Tower. After they had been shown the vault holding the jewels the 'clergyman's' wife complained of a violent stomach ache and was taken to the apartments above to be looked after by the keeper's wife. Returning a few days later with a gift of white gloves for Mrs Edwards to thank her for her kindness, the two couples soon struck up a friendship, which allowed the plotters to check out the Tower thoroughly and come and go without remark.

On 9 May 1671 the clergyman arrived at the Martin Tower with two young men, one purporting to be his nephew, whom he'd brought along as a potential suitor for the daughter of Mr and Mrs Edwards. Arriving early on purpose, while the ladies of the house were still getting ready, Blood asked Edwards to show his nephew the Crown Jewels in the strong room below, as a way of passing the time. Once in the basement the nephew overpowered Edwards, who was in his 70s, and swiftly bound, gagged and beat him. The three men set about carrying off the treasure. They had planned well: Blood had brought along a mallet to squash the state crown until it was flat enough to be hidden under his cloak, while one accomplice, wearing baggy breeches for the purpose, shoved the Orb down his trousers. The other prepared to saw the Sceptre in half, as they realised it was too long and distinctive to be disguised and carried away successfully.

Blood and his gang would have succeeded had the Edwards's son not unexpectedly arrived home – an unforeseen event since he had been away fighting in Flanders for several years. The thieves tried to escape but were overpowered by the Yeoman Warders which Edwards had summoned (see page 97).

A DISPLAY OF WEALTH

Like the Royal Menagerie, the Crown Jewels became an early tourist attraction at the Tower. They were also a way for the ruler to show off their wealth and were often displayed for visiting dignitaries and important visitors, initially with the monarch present. When the king of Denmark made a ceremonial visit to James I in 1606, part of the entertainment laid on was to go to the Tower where 'to their Kingly presence in the Jewell-house were presented the most rare and richest jewels and beawtifull plate, so that he might wonder thereat, but cannot truly prayse or estimate the value thereof by many thousands of pounds.' The visiting king could not have begun to estimate the actual worth of what he was seeing, but he was dazzled, which was the point.

When the Jewels were first displayed to the public, they were kept in wooden-slatted cages, and visitors were encouraged to reach between the slats to feel them. 'It would be possible to get ones hand through and pick up the articles to feel their weight,' one visitor noted. When William Hutton visited the Tower in the 1780s he was invited to handle the pieces and also offered the opportunity to try on the royal bracelets and spurs. One woman, described in reports as 'mad', pushed down the arches of one of the crowns. Following Colonel Blood's attempt to steal the Crown Jewels, they were finally enclosed with ornate iron grillework which was kept firmly locked.

Visitors to the Crown Jewels increased considerably in Victorian times, and the Master of the Jewel House, Edmund Lenthal Swifte, claimed a salary for his cleaning lady as a tour guide, although by all accounts her knowledge of the displays

Who was Colonel Blood?

This notorious, if engaging rogue, was born in County Clare, Ireland in 1618, but came to England at an early age. During the Civil War he sided with the Parliamentarians and was granted a large estate 'for services rendered' – which, many have speculated, included espionage. With the restoration of the monarchy, Blood, now styling himself 'Colonel', lost his lands and fled to Ireland with his wife and son. There he joined disgruntled Cromwellian supporters in a failed attempt to kidnap the Duke of Ormonde, Lord Lieutenant of Ireland. His escapade with the Crown Jewels in 1671 might have succeeded had chance, in the shape of Talbot Edwards' son, not intervened. During his trial Blood maintained he would answer to no one but the king and, amazingly, Charles II granted him an audience. Soon after, for reasons unknown, Blood received a pardon, not only for the attempt on the Crown Jewels but for any other 'indiscretions' that might come to light later, and also got back his income from the land grants.

This majesterial largesse has led some historians to speculate whether Blood had actually been sent by the king to steal the jewels – war and the cost of re-establishing the monarchy in high style had left the royal treasury bare. Others have suggested that Blood's resolute attempts to kidnap the Duke of Ormonde were at the behest of the king's chief minister. Blood died on 24 August 1680. His epitaph read: 'Here lies the man who boldly hath run through/More villanies than England ever knew,' hinting at secret skulduggery or espionage at a high level.

> The Coronation Ring was **too large for Queen Victoria** and so a smaller one was made for her coronation in 1838. It was incorrectly made to fit her little finger, and the Archbishop had to force the ring on to her fourth finger.
> Queen Victoria later noted in her diary:
> **'I had the greatest difficulty to take if off again – which at last I did with great pain.'**

was extremely limited. The Lord Chamberlain felt that someone who knew more about the collection should be selected and in 1851 appointed Ann Richardson as Exhibitor. Lenthal Swifte was required to provide board and lodgings for the new guide, which led to a very uncomfortable situation, as Mrs Swifte refused to clean Ann Richardson's room and told the servants not to obey her. Later that year Lenthal Swifte resigned, after 38 years of looking after the royal displays. Women continued to hold the post of Exhibitor until 1900, when it was abolished and replaced by a Curator.

Lenthal Swifte contributed a great deal by way of security, but his care almost caused disaster during the fire in the Grand Storehouse in 1841 (see Chapter 2). The keys to the jewel cases were not found to be within the Tower precincts, so the iron bars had to be bent by brute force, and the Jewels pulled out by a medley of helpers while the fire next door crept closer. As *The Times* reported the next day: 'A most extraordinary scene presented itself, the warders carrying crowns, sceptres and other valuables of royalty, between groups of soldiers, police, firemen and others from the Jewel Tower to the Governors residence.'

By the 19th century it had long been recognised that the lower Martin Tower was too cramped and dingy to display the Crown Jewels properly. William Hutton, writing in *A Journey from Birmingham to London* in 1784, had thought it 'a dismal hole, resembling the cell of the condemned. Two wretched candles just lighted up, added to the gloom'. New candle lamps were installed in the 1820s, then oil lamps in 1833, and some items, such as the intricate Exeter Salt, were placed on revolving stands and put in glass cases to make them visible on all sides. But the effect was still unsatisfactory. By 1840 work was underway on a dedicated building that was designed to take advantage of natural light and to show the Crown Jewels at their best. They were moved in 1842, but unfortunately the new building was badly designed and proved to be just as dim as its predecessor. Not only was the building dark, but it was not fire proof, was impossible to secure properly, and was permanently damp – a disaster in every way! Despite a number of alterations and improvements, in 1852, the Duke of Wellington, who was Constable of the Tower, declared that it had to go.

Eventually, in 1870, the Crown Jewels moved to the first floor of the Wakefield Tower, which allowed for better display and security in the form of ornate 12ft-high cases. Apartments were created for the Keeper in St Thomas's Tower, and the two were linked by a bridge. As the century progressed, more items were added to the displays, such as the state trumpets, with their intricately stitched banners, and some spectacular maces.

The Crown Jewels stayed in the Wakefield Tower for almost a century, except when they were hastily packed and evacuated in just nine days before the outbreak of World War II. They were

For the **coronation of George VI in 1937**, the king, fearing the Archbishop might not be able to distinguish the front of St Edward's Crown from the back, had arranged for the front to be marked with a small piece of red cotton. However, the cotton was somehow removed and the crown was put on the king's head **back to front**.

kept at Westwood Quarry, in Wiltshire, along with many of Britain's other art treasures.

The final major move of the Crown Jewels took place in 1967, when the basement of the Waterloo Barracks was refitted to accommodate them. They were brought upstairs in 1994, and informative film shows were added to explain the history and use of the Crown Jewels. With over 2.5 million people wanting to see the Crown Jewels every year, a moving walkway now provides the only way to keep pedestrian traffic moving at the most popular times, a sign that the exhibition really has entered the 21st century.

CHAPTER

IMPRISONMENT

he Tower received its first prisoner in 1100 and its last in 1941. In between those years, some 8,000 people were incarcerated within its walls for crimes ranging from conspiracy, murder and high treason, to debt, sorcery and speaking unwisely at the wrong time. Some were held for a few days; some for many years. Some of the more important prisoners lived in quite luxurious style, with their own furnishings, well-stocked larders and with servants and sometimes even family members staying with them. Most of this would be at their own expense. At the other end of the scale, though, there are records of prisoners housed in rat-infested cellars and storerooms, stables and converted corridors with only very basic necessities and food.

The cold reality in Medieval England was that the imprisonment and occasional murder of a political rival was not uncommon. Nowhere is this more obvious than in the fates of Henry VI and the sons of his rival, Edward IV.

Henry was a mere infant when he became king in 1422, and at his coming of age, he inherited a kingdom riven by strife thanks to the Wars of the Roses (see Chapter 1). In 1461, Henry lost the crown, partly as a result of military weakness and partly as a result of the House of York's ambitions. Forced to shelter in Scotland for five years, Henry was eventually betrayed into the hands of his royal rival, soon to become Edward IV, and was packed off to the Tower. The terms of his confinement were not as harsh as they might have been, for he was allowed to attend mass, and Edward IV spent enormous sums of money on retainers, food and drink for his predecessor – and, briefly, his successor, because in an improbable twist of fate, Henry

When **King John Baliol of Scotland** was
imprisoned by Edward I at the end of the
13th century he brought with him:

Master William, a chaplain

Henry, chapel clerk

Several assistants for Henry

Master Andrew, a tailor

One laundress

Two squires

Three pages

Two chamberlains

One barber

One huntsman

Two grooms

One pledgeman [who stood surety for his return while
he was allowed to go out hunting!]

10 hunting dogs

Two greyhounds

In his *A Child's History of England*, Charles Dickens
describes the exiled king's incarceration as rather a good thing:
'Baliol had the Tower of London lent him for a residence, with
permission to range about within a circle of twenty miles.
Three years afterwards he was allowed to go to Normandy,
where he had estates, and where he passed the remaining six
years of his life: far more happily, I dare say, than he
had lived for a long while in angry Scotland.'

suddenly found himself back on the throne again in 1470, albeit as a tool of Richard Neville, Earl of Warwick. Warwick, 'The Kingmaker', planned a marriage for his daughter with Henry's eldest son, yet a mere six months later, Henry's supporters were defeated again and Henry was back in the Tower. Here, rumour has it, he was killed soon after by a hardened Edward IV, who was prepared to take no further chances of Henry becoming a figurehead for a rebellion. This luckless and rather sensitive monarch is remembered annually at the Ceremony of Lilies and Roses (see Chapter 8).

Seven years after Henry VI's suspicious demise, Edward IV's own brother met a very questionable end in the Tower. Canadian author Thomas B Costain gives a rather breathless description of the legendary death of the Duke of Clarence in *The Last Plantagenets*: 'With public curiosity at boiling point, it was impossible to conceal the fact that the sentence had been carried out on the seventeenth or eighteenth of February. But then a curious story began to circulate, to pass from mouth to mouth, to fill the minds of all people with fascinated horror, to set the customers in taverns into goggle-eyed speculation over their ale. Clarence, at his own request, had been drowned in a butt of the rare wine called malmsey.'

The death of Edward IV soon after, in 1483, set in motion events leading up to one of the Tower's most famous tales... The story of the Princes in the Tower is a celebrated favourite. The boys in question were Edward IV's young sons, Edward V and Richard, Duke of York; they were allegedly murdered while living at the Tower. There are a number of theories, the leading one being that they were killed at the behest of their uncle and

'This day I, standing by the opening, saw workmen dig out of a stairway in the White Tower, the bones of those two Princes who were foully murdered by **Richard III**... they were small bones, of lads in their teens and there were pieces of rag and velvet about them... Being fully recognised to be the bones of those two Princes they were carefully put aside in a stone coffin or coffer.'

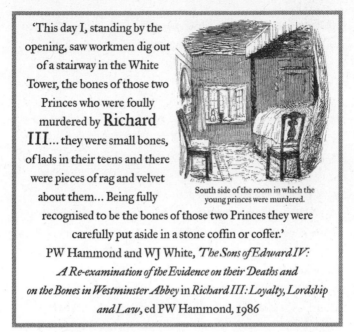

South side of the room in which the young princes were murdered.

PW Hammond and WJ White, *The Sons of Edward IV: A Re-examination of the Evidence on their Deaths and on the Bones in Westminster Abbey* in *Richard III: Loyalty, Lordship and Law*, ed PW Hammond, 1986

protector, Richard of Gloucester, who was crowned as Richard III (1483-1485) in 1483. Supporters of Richard (there is a thriving Richard III Society) argue that this story arose when Henry Tudor took the throne from Richard III and needed to besmirch Richard's name to strengthen his own claim. Detractors point to Richard's overwhelming opportunity and motive – a classic murder mystery that may never be completely solved.

In 1674, nearly 200 years after the murder – or disappearance, at least – of the Princes in the Tower, the skeletons of two young boys were found near the White Tower. Questions have since been raised about their identity, but at the time Charles II had no doubt that these were the poignant remains of the slaughtered Edward and Richard and duly had them interred in Westminster Abbey.

EQUAL OPPORTUNITIES

The Tower welcomed women prisoners as freely as it did men. Anne Boleyn and Lady Jane Grey are perhaps the most famous, but not the only women, or the only queens, to have been taken there as a prisoner, and the Tower's female inmates – nobles, heretics, rivals to the throne or victims of circumstance – have caught our attention as some of the most colourful women in British history.

The Tower's first recorded female prisoner was Margaret de Clare, Lady Badlesmere of Leeds Castle. When Edward II's Queen Isabella, en route for Canterbury, stopped and asked for a night's lodging, the fiery owner not only gave the Queen short shrift, but also killed the messenger who had the temerity to make the request. In response, Edward took Leeds Castle by force and threw Lady Badlesmere in the Tower.

The Bloody Tower was originally called The Garden Tower. Its association with the deaths of the Princes in the Tower prompted the less cheery name.

> '**Oh, Lord!** I never thought to have come here as
> a prisoner; and I pray you all good friends and fellows,
> bear me witness that I come in no traitor, but as true a
> woman to the Queen's Majesty as any is now living, and
> thereon will I take my death.'
>
> *Elizabeth I's words when, as princess, she alighted – probably at*
> *the Byward Postern rather than Traitor's Gate – following Sir*
> *Thomas Wyatt's uprising in 1554.*

The Tower also imprisoned before execution the elderly
Countess of Salisbury, Margaret Pole (the last surviving
Plantagenet princess), Henry VIII's second and fifth wives, Anne
Boleyn and Catherine Howard, and Lady Jane Grey (see Chapter
7). On Palm Sunday 1554, the Tower received another royal
female prisoner: the 21-year-old future Queen Elizabeth.

In typically high style, Queen Elizabeth rebuffed her
attainder for high treason, declaring upon entering the gates:
'Here landeth as true a subject, being prisoner, as ever landed
at these stairs; and before thee, O God, I speak it, having no
friends but thee alone.'

As Elizabeth was the daughter of Anne Boleyn, the woman
who had replaced her own mother, Queen Mary could never
reconcile herself to Elizabeth's claim to legitimacy. On her
orders, a series of investigations and interrogations sought to
implicate the Princess in Sir Thomas Wyatt's conspiracy to
prevent the marriage of Mary I and King Philip of Spain,
installing Elizabeth in her stead. No proof was found and
Elizabeth was released two months later.

CONSPIRACY FOR THE CROWN

Sir Walter Ralegh was one of the most flamboyant men of his age, but paid the price of being both a favourite of Queen Elizabeth I and an enemy of James I. He was imprisoned in the Tower on no less than three occasions.

When Ralegh first encountered the ageing queen at Greenwich in 1581, she was clearly captivated by him. She knighted him and honoured him with the title Captain of the Guard. However, when Ralegh secretly married her Maid of Honour, Elizabeth Throckmorton, the queen sent him to the Tower in a fit of pique – he was released five weeks later when she had cooled down.

His second incarceration was much more serious. On 14 July 1603 the new King James I had Ralegh arrested for involvement with a conspiracy to place the crown on the head of Lady Arbella Stuart. This was treason and a hopeless cause, as Ralegh knew, and while awaiting trial he attempted to commit suicide by stabbing himself with a kitchen knife. Soon afterwards, he was condemned to death, but the sentence was revoked to life imprisonment.

This sentence for such a lusty and active man as Ralegh must have been very hard. As small compensation, the Bloody Tower, in which he was held, was enlarged to accommodate his family. Indeed, his second son, Carew, was born in the Tower in 1605. Ralegh was allowed to move freely around the Tower precincts and to use part of the Lieutenant's Garden, even exercising on the raised wall between the two buildings, which is now known as Ralegh's

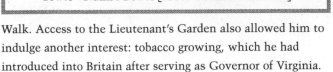

Towers which were designated suitable for use as prisons in 1641 included: The Cradle Tower • The Well Tower • Salt Tower • Broad Arrow Tower • Constable Tower • Martin Tower • Beauchamp Tower • Bell Tower • Wakefield Tower • Lanthorn Tower • Nunn's Bower [above Coldharbour Gate]

Walk. Access to the Lieutenant's Garden also allowed him to indulge another interest: tobacco growing, which he had introduced into Britain after serving as Governor of Virginia.

As a prisoner of rank, Ralegh was permitted to have three servants, but this service did not come free – prisoners at the Tower were expected to pay their way. This privileged form of imprisonment allowed Ralegh to write extensively, and he began a history of the world, which was never completed; the first volume only was published in 1614. In filling his days with busy industry and exercise, he might have been following the example of earlier prisoners. Hugh Draper, for example, who was incarcerated as a suspected sorcerer in 1561, carved an incredibly intricate astronomical clock, which can still be seen to this day on the walls of his room in the Salt Tower.

Apart from gardening and writing, Ralegh occupied his time with chemical experiments, ingeniously converting a small hen house into a laboratory. He became convinced that he possessed the information necessary to find the fabled city of 'El Dorado' and all the riches that it contained. In 1616, he negotiated a temporary release to pursue this quest.

The Crown may have hoped that the errant knight would never return, but the expedition failed and the quixotic Ralegh and his men attacked the Spanish settlement of St Thomas. He returned to face his third stay in the Tower, under sentence of death at the insistence of the Spanish minister, the Conde de Gondomar. The adventurer was finally executed on 29 October

The imprisonment of Sir Thomas More

Famous prisoners held in the Tower:

The Kray twins, East End gangsters · **Jean II,** King of France, following his defeat at Poitiers in 1356 · **Elizabeth I,** before she became Queen of England · **Rudolf Hess,** Nazi Deputy Führer · **Walter Ralegh,** pirate and courtier · **Sir Thomas More,** Catholic Chancellor · **Edmund Campion,** Jesuit theologian · **Lady Jane Grey,** Queen of England for nine days · **Anne Boleyn,** Queen of England · **Catherine Howard,** Queen of England · **Guy Fawkes** and his fellow conspirators

1618 in Old Palace Yard in Westminster, after reaching out to feel the blade of the axe and declaring: 'Tis a sharp remedy but a sure cure for all ills.'

The case of the murdered poet and essayist Sir Thomas Overbury is an unusual example of a prisoner who should have been safe in the Tower – but wasn't.

As a youth, Overbury travelled to join his great friend Robert Carr, a page at court. Both men rose quickly at court, due to their good looks and James I's weakness for pretty young men. Carr acquired the title of Lord Rochester, while Overbury was knighted. Rochester then became hopelessly infatuated with a notorious young woman, the Countess of Essex. Although only 17, she was worldly enough to divorce her first husband (she had married at 13) in favour of Rochester. Overbury strongly opposed the match, reputedly telling his friend on one occasion: 'My lord, if you do marry that filthy, base woman, you will utterly ruin your honour and yourself.'

The insulted Countess immediately began to spin a plot to secure Overbury's downfall, and not long after he was sent to the Tower on a charge of insulting the Crown. She then began the final phase of her plot to eliminate her rival – she began to poison him with the aid of two apothecaries, Franklin and Weston (Weston had obtained the position of Keeper of the Tower at the Countess's instigation). The poisons, which included a compound of arsenic, rosalger, sublimate of mercury and white arsenic, were served to Overbury daily in his food, and administered so slowly and carefully that the initial cause of death four months later was thought to be syphilis, due to the excessive blisters and abrasions on his

> Christopher Wren's uncle, **Matthew Wren, Bishop of Ely** was arrested in 1642 during the Civil War and spent 18 years in the Tower of London without being tried or convicted of any crime. He was held under suspicion of storing ammunition for the Royalists.

skin. However, the villains were brought to justice when medical witnesses were called to prove the cause of death. Franklin testified that he was unaware of the purpose of the purchased poison and Weston pleaded his innocence throughout, but both were hanged. Rochester and the Countess were found guilty of murder and sentenced to death, but this was retracted.

As lucky as they were wicked, after five years in the Tower, they were given licence to remain in the grounds of a country house and received a full pardon from the king four years later.

THE GREAT ESCAPES

The Tower of London has always had a reputation for being pretty much impregnable, but several hardy souls have still succeeded in escaping its walls.

The first of these escapees was, ironically, the Tower's very first prisoner. Bishop Ranulf Flambard, the Bishop of Durham, was incarcerated there in 1100 for extortion. After a year-long comfortable and luxurious stay, Flambard gulled the guards royally by throwing a party for them at which they became so inebriated they failed to notice his absence. The bishop, who must have been reasonably limber for his age, took rope which had been smuggled in to him concealed in a wine casket and lowered himself down the outer wall of the Tower.

When the rope proved to be several feet too short, he jumped down, mercifully breaking no bones, and fled to a boat that was waiting on the river for him. (In contrast to some later monarchs, who executed supposed traitors as a matter of expedience on the flimsiest evidence, Henry pardoned Ranulf and restored him to his bishopric.)

If Flambard's escape is one of the most robust and athletic, the tale of the Jesuit priest Father John Gerard's escape shows the most cunning. While Gerard was imprisoned in the Salt Tower in 1587, he persuaded a helpful jailor to bring him oranges, at the time a rare and costly fruit. Gerard wasn't worried about his diet, though; he wanted the juice, with which he could write secret messages that were invisible when dry.

This ingenious method allowed Gerard to carry on an active correspondence with supporters on the outside, and also to contact a fellow prisoner, John Arden, in the Cradle Tower. Together, Gerard and Arden contrived to get a guard to let them celebrate mass together and used their regular meetings to hatch a plot. On 5 October 1587, Gerard and Arden descended from the Cradle Tower, swung across the moat on a rope and landed in a boat waiting on the Thames below.

> The longest serving prisoner was Sir William de la Pole, a distant relative of Henry VII, who was incarcerated in the Tower for 37 years [1502-1539] for allegedly plotting to seize the throne.

The final – and in many ways most outlandish – escape on record occurred in 1716. William Maxwell, Lord Nithsdale, eschewing the derring-do of escapees who'd scaled walls and shinned across ropes, took a much more direct route out of the Tower. Nithsdale had been captured and imprisoned in the first Jacobite Rising of 1715, and was languishing in the Lieutenant's Lodgings on the eve of his execution, when he had a visit from his wife, Lady Nithsdale. Unaware that a reprieve had been signed that evening, and determined at all costs to save her husband, Lady Nithsdale and her friends brought him a disguise of women's clothing. Lord Nithsdale simply dressed as a woman and walked out past the guards, leaving his wife in his place in the cell. On hearing of his escape, George I (1714-1727) is said to have remarked: 'It is the best that a man in his situation could have done.' While Nithsdale travelled on to Rome, disguised as a servant of the Venetian ambassador, his wife coolly returned

---

Some were imprisoned in the Tower for the most unusual crimes...

Johan Wheler, imprisoned in 1554 for saying that King Edward VI was still alive.

Thomas Fleete, imprisoned in 1662 for making an 'incautious remark' during the loading of a ship.

Sir John Towers, imprisoned in September 1665 accused of forging the king's signature.

Theophilus Hastings, 7th Earl of Huntington, imprisoned in May 1692 under suspicion of high treason due to the large number of horses he kept in his stables.

Being imprisoned in the Tower for his writings in February 1633 didn't dissuade **Puritan dissident William Prynne** from producing several more works. To be fair, having his ears cut off or having his face branded with the letters **SL for Seditious Libeller** didn't either. Despite having been imprisoned for publishing books denouncing the church and the lax morals of the court, Prynne was allowed free access to information and pens and paper – evidently quite a lot of paper because while in prison he wrote *A Breviate of the Prelates Intollerable Usurpations*, *The Unbishoping of Timothy* and *Titus and Briefe Instructions for Churchwardens*, all of which were smuggled out by his frequent visitors and published anonymously.

to Dumfriesshire for their possessions and then joined him in Rome, where they resided for 33 years.

THE WAR YEARS

During World War I, captured spies were held on trial in the Tower and executed by firing squad on Tower Hill (see Chapter 7). The Irish revolutionary Sir Roger Casement was also an inmate in 1916, pending trial after he was charged with visiting Irish prisoners-of-war in Germany and persuading them to form an Irish brigade of the German army.

During World War II, the Tower was pressed into service again, and nearly 180 prisoners, included the 43-strong crew of U-boat 39, were temporarily held in the New Armouries, the Main Guard building north of the Wakefield Tower and the hospital before being moved on.

> Towers in which **prisoners left inscriptions**, some lengthy and inspiring, others cyphers of their names [it depended, we imagine, on how long they were incarcerated, some managed to carve out paragraphs!]:
> **Bloody Tower, Beauchamp Tower, Martin Tower, Salt Tower** and **Broad Arrow Tower**

Occasionally a big-name prisoner would arrive, causing a flurry of nervous excitement. The first of these, in 1940, was Doctor Herr Gerlach, an ardent Nazi and German Consul General to Iceland, who was arrested after being caught burning key documents in Reykjavik. Gerlach was taken to the Tower on 11 June 1940, and during his three-month stay in the King's House (now the Queen's House) he befriended the four-year-old son of a Yeoman Warder.

The most famous Nazi prisoner to be interned in the Tower of London, albeit even more briefly, was Rudolph Hess, Germany's Deputy Führer. Hess had been flying his own ME 110D over Scotland and was forced to bail out. He was captured and taken to the Tower on 17 May 1941, where he remained for just four days – long enough to commit his autograph to a piece of Tower stationery now framed in the Yeoman Warders' club. It was always a mystery as to why he had ventured into enemy territory on his own account, and his trial at Nuremberg in 1945 did not shed any light on the matter. Hess ended his days in Spandau Prison, dying in 1987.

CHAPTER

7

TORTURE &
EXECUTION

he dreaded order of 'Off to the Tower' is inexorably linked in the popular imagination with dank dungeons and the screams of tortured souls ringing out daily from the rack and other such scourges. Folk tales, thrilling dramas and Hollywood films have all helped fuel this image, but just how realistic is it?

Such a terrifying reputation would undoubtedly have served as a useful deterrent. It was certainly not discouraged, but historical records actually reveal the truth. Very few people were tortured at the Tower of London. There wasn't a huge dungeon full of sinister-looking instruments presided over by a hunch-backed sadist waving a selection of branding irons. From the side of the torturers, there are very few accounts, and those that do exist tend to be matter-of-fact records of methods employed and information gleaned. On the victim's part, the accounts tend to be more gut-wrenching, but those who did survive and wrote down their experiences tended to be from the literate upper class who had found themselves imprisoned due to political or religious affiliation, or court intrigue, and possibly exaggerated their experiences to further their cause.

> **Medieval folk legend** built up the Tower's image as a place of horror and despair, and Shakespeare describes it as an awful place, but the common image was undoubtedly fixed by *The Tower of London*, a lurid romance of 1840 by W Harrison Ainsworth. Ainsworth's work, which was extremely popular in its day, is full of sinister, scheming ministers, sadistic torturers and deformed guards.

Of the **48 warrants** for torture carried out at the Tower during the Tudor and Stuart periods, **11** were to extract information about robbery, which ranged from horse rustling to **breaking into Windsor Castle**. There were **14 prisoners** tortured about sedition, **nine** about treason and **nine** about matters simply described as **'religion'**.

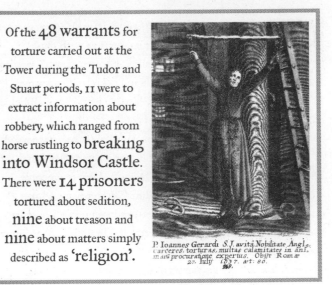

P. Ioannes Gerardi S.J. avitâ Nobilitate Angl.
Carceres, torturas, multas calamitates in Ani.
in arâ procuratione expertus. Obijt Romæ
27. Iulij 1637. æt: 80.

Popular conception also identifies torture with treason, political plotting and heresy. It's true that the 16th and 17th centuries were a period of political instability and, following Henry VIII's break with the Catholic Church, changeable religious orientation, which led to vicious denunciation, accusation and counter-accusation. But the Tower's records show some of the people sent to be tortured had committed comparatively minor crimes like robbery or stealing horses.

Most instances of torture at the Tower took place during the reigns of the Tudors and Stuarts, although it was first legally sanctioned during the Templar trials of the early-14th century, when Edward II was on the throne. There are few accounts of this type of interrogation, however, throughout the Middle Ages – England largely resisted the Inquisition, and there simply

> The **Spanish Armoury collection** – supposedly captured from the Armada of 1588, but actually dating from much earlier [see Chapter 2] – contains **thumbscrews, spiked collars and bilbos** [iron gauntlets which crushed the fingers]. It would be naive to assume the king had those just **lying around for decoration…**

doesn't seem to have been an established tradition of torturing people for information. Although torture later became an acknowledged tool of the judicial system in England, it was never formally sanctioned as part of English Law. It could only be ordered by the Privy Council by special warrant, which gave immunity to those officers who carried it out.

Torture was not supposed to be used to obtain a confession, but rather to extract additional information about accomplices or plots from those whose guilt was already proven. If you knew you were going to die a horrible death, there was very little incentive to implicate anyone else.

A TORTUROUS PROCESS

The first actual record of official torture taking place at the Tower of London dates back to 1539, when an unnamed Irish monk, presumably Catholic, was stretched on the brake, an early name for the rack. A year later, Thomas Thwaytes was sent to the Tower and was ordered to be sent to the brake if he didn't confess. There is no record of whether or not Thomas was actually racked.

There were two types of people involved in a torture session (apart from the victim, of course): those who asked the questions and those who operated the machinery. The physical side of the torture was carried out by Yeoman Warders, at the direction of the Lieutenant of the Tower. But the questioning was done by two or three Commissioners, one of whom was usually an officer of the court, such as the Royal Attorney or Royal Solicitor. The officers of the court present would all have been sent a letter of instruction, such as this one of 13 April 1597 directed to Sir Richard Barkley, Lieutenant of the Tower, Mr Solicitor, Mr Bacon and William Waad, who later became Lieutenant of the Tower (1603-1613), authorising the interrogation of a Jesuit priest (possibly John Gerard): 'These shall be therefore to require you to examine him strictly upon such interrogatories as shall be fit to be ministered unto him and he ought to answer to manifest the truth in that behalf and other things that may concern Her Majesty and the State, wherein if you find him obstinate, undutiful or unwilling to declare and reveal the truth as he ought to do by his duty and allegiance, you shall by such venture hereof cause him to be put to the manacles and such other torture as is used in that place, that he may be forced to utter directly and truly his uttermost knowledge in all things that may any way concern Her Majesty and the State and are meet to be known.'

Some officers of the court obliged to examine prisoners under torture found it a very difficult task. Following the torture of John Gerard, Sir Richard Berkeley, then Lieutenant of the Tower, resigned, saying he couldn't face being involved in such activity again. Others, however, took pleasure in their job and enjoyed it. Richard Topcliffe, Recorder of London, became the most notorious interrogator of Elizabethan England, and travelled the country wringing confessions out of Catholic prisoners, even though it was not his job to do so. He enjoyed applying the instruments of torture as much as asking the questions, overriding the usual strict distinction drawn between the interrogator and the more lowly enforcer. On one occasion, Topcliffe tortured the Jesuit Robert Southwell in his house by hanging him from the manacles. He then went out and forgot all about his prisoner. Southwell was only saved from death by one of Topcliffe's servants.

The Tower's dreaded reputation, and a not unnatural fear of pain, often allowed interrogators to get information without actually having to hurt anyone. A prisoner would first be taken to a dark dungeon, shown the instruments of torture and have described to them what was going to happen. John Gerard recounted being introduced to the Master of Torture by the Clerk of the Council, whose job it was to extract his confession. He later learned the Master of Torture was just an ordinary soldier dressed up to frighten him.

The location of the chamber used for torture is something of a mystery. Possibly it was located in the basement of the old Flint Tower, which was sometimes referred to as Little Hell, or the White Tower itself, where the Cannon Room is now – it had

> **The rack** was sometimes known as the **Duke of Exeter's Daughter** because it was supposed to have been invented by John Holland, Duke of Exeter, who held the role of Constable of the Tower [1446-1447].

a wooden ceiling like that described by John Gerard, and at various times was used as a prison or storeroom. The few descriptions of the route to the torture chamber suggest that prisoners were taken through a series of underground tunnels and their locations are now lost.

THE RACK

The rack, the main device used for extracting information, was not a new instrument of torture: the same principle had been used by the Greeks and Romans, and the design had been modified throughout the Middle Ages.

Early types of rack had two separate rollers at either end, or a single roller which caused the arms or legs to be pulled while the other limbs were fastened in place. The more sophisticated model, which was the version eventually introduced to the Tower had a central roller attached to a ratchet, with ropes leading to two end rollers, so the motion of the single central roller caused the other rollers to move in opposite directions, stretching the victim even further.

The rack was regarded as a desirable form of torture from an inquisitor's point of view, because it was precise and measured, the ratchet device allowing the ropes or chains to be tightened in small increments, and the victim left at a particular stretch for a period without their becoming slack.

Equally, inquisitors knew that the pain of the rack was much worse on the second or third application, and that someone who had steadfastly refused to give up information after a severe first application might spill the beans very swiftly on a second.

The gratynge of an arrowe thpoughe Cuthbert Simons fyngers.

Cuthbert Simson vpon the racke.

The description howe Cuthbert Simson ftode in an engyne of yron three houres, within the Tower, comonlye called Scevyngtons Glove.

Cuthbert Simpson, a Protestant deacon, was imprisoned in **the Tower** during the reign of the **Catholic Queen Mary I**, accused of heresy. He was tortured on the rack and with the Scavenger's Daughter. He was finally burned at **Smithfield** in March 1558.

Catholic conspirator Francis Throckmorton refused resolutely to give information of a plot against Elizabeth I on his first stretching, but afterwards it was recorded that the 'grief of the last torture will suffice without any extremity of racking to make him more conformable'.

In 1628, a legal challenge to the use of the rack was mounted. The Privy Council wanted to examine John Felton, who had assassinated the Duke of Buckingham in August of that year, after a disastrous campaign to provoke a Huguenot uprising in France had been followed by an embarrassing climb down and a peace treaty. The court declared that use of the rack was contrary to British law. Blackstone wrote: 'When, upon the assassination of George Villiers, 1st Duke of Buckingham, by John Felton, it was proposed in the Privy Council to put the assassin to the rack, in order to discover his accomplices, the judges being consulted, declared unanimously that no such proceeding was allowable by the laws of England.'

THE SCAVENGER'S DAUGHTER

The Scavenger's Daughter, invented by Leonard Skeffington, Lieutenant of the Tower during Henry VIII's tenure on the throne, compressed its victim, rather than stretched them. It would appear that inventing torture instruments seemed to have been a gentlemanly hobby for Tower officials.

There is, however, some confusion about the construction of the Scavenger's Daughter, because depictions in Foxe's *Book of Martyrs* of Cuthbert Simpson being interrogated include a triangular set of rigid irons which imprisoned feet, neck and wrists in what was a bent, but fundamentally upright, position. This was not crushing the body as the Scavenger's Daughter was reported to do. This arrangement was sometimes called Skeffington's Gyves. An illustration from a guide to the Tower in 1820 shows a young and rather cheerful Yeoman Warder displaying them to a visiting family, and since no actual Scavenger's Daughter remained in the collection, the mix-up was understandable.

The real Scavenger's Daughter, by contrast, a replica of which can now been seen at the Tower, consisted of a circular plate of metal on which the prisoner was made to kneel with their head down and arms close by their sides. Fixed to either side of it were curved, ascending bars, similar in shape to that of a wishbone, which could be drawn closer and closer together over the top of a prisoner's back by means of a screw. As they closed, they had the effect of forcing the torso down onto the calves and thighs, and the arms in against the ribcage until bones slowly snapped and internal organs were crushed by the pressure of the victim's own body. The name comes, presumably, from the enforced position being reminiscent of someone crouching to forage or scavenge.

There are very few accounts of the Scavenger's Daughter being used. Two Catholic priests, Luke Kirby and Thomas Cottam, were subjected to it in December 1580. They both confessed after an hour.

THE MANACLES

Unlike the Rack or Scavenger's Daughter, the manacles did less immediate damage, and could be employed for a period of hours. Father John Gerard, a Jesuit from Rome, offers us a detailed and descriptive account of how they were used.

Gerard was imprisoned by Queen Elizabeth I for three years before being taken to the Tower, where he was tortured in an effort to extract the identity of the leader of the Catholic spy ring with which he was alleged to have been involved. Father Gerard had survived for six years disguising himself as a gentleman of leisure and travelling around the country, secretly ministering to Catholics. The other three Jesuits who had snuck

> 'None was put to the rack that was not at first by some manifest evidence known to the Council to be guilty of treason, so that it was well assured beforehand that there was no innocent tormented. Also none was tormented to know whether he was guilty or no, but for the Queen's safety to know the manner of the treason and the accomplices.'
>
> *Francis Walshingham, Elizabeth I's Secretary of State and loyal intriguer,* 1582

into the country with him had fared less well, and had all been caught and executed by then.

Gerard is famous for his escape from the Tower (see Chapter 6), after which he spent another eight years in hiding until the Gunpowder Plot was uncovered before being smuggled out of the country as part of a Spanish diplomatic mission. In a book he later wrote, called *The Autobiography of an Elizabethan*, Gerard described his experience of torture at the Tower: 'My arms were then lifted up and an iron bar was passed through the rings of one gauntlet, then through the staple and rings to the second gauntlet. This done, they fastened the bar with a pin to prevent it from slipping, and then, removing the wicker steps one by one from under my feet, they left me hanging by my hands and arms fastened above my head... Hanging like this I began to pray. The gentlemen standing around me asked me whether I was willing to confess now. "I cannot and I will not," I answered. But I could hardly utter the words, such a gripping pain came over me. It was worst in my chest and belly, my hands and arms. All the blood in my body seemed to rush up into my arms and hands and I thought that blood was oozing from the ends of my fingers and the pores of my skin.'

Gerard was hung in the manacles all day, being supported every time he fainted until he could be brought round to prolong his pain (around eight or nine times by his account) until the clock struck five and he was taken down, without revealing anything. Perhaps because they allowed for longer questioning with less severe after-effects, once the manacles were introduced to the Tower (the first account of their use was in 1591) they were the most frequently used method of persuasion. Another Jesuit priest, Henry Walpole, is recorded as having been hung in the manacles no less than 14 times. He recovered from temporary numbness in his hands, although friends noted his ability to write neatly was forever ruined.

Torture sometimes worked, and sometimes it didn't. Edmund Campion, the Catholic martyr, was interrogated three times in 1581 without giving up any details on other Catholics. Guy Fawkes, following his involvement in the attempt to blow up the Houses of Parliament, eventually confessed and confirmed the names of all his co-conspirators. It's not known if Fawkes was racked, but historians often cite the difference between his scrawled and shaky signature on the documents of confession and his signature during the early days of his imprisonment.

The last official record of torture is dated 1640, when John Archer, who had attacked Archbishop Laud's palace, was questioned about accomplices. The rack remained in awful readiness until 1673, but after 33 years gathering cobwebs, the decision was taken to move it to the Grand Storehouse.

Anne Boleyn's brother, George, Viscount Rochford, wound up incarcerated and later beheaded because he'd been seen **putting his hand on his sister's bed** while talking with her, in full view of all her attendants. Incredibly this was classified as incest by a court all too eager to please Henry VIII.

When torture fell out of favour as a judicial tool, the instruments that had been feared became objects of curiosity. Today, torture instruments that had been stored for posterity by the Office of the Ordnance, with a replica of the rack, make up part of an exhibition that attempts to re-educate the public on what did and didn't happen in the Tower's chambers of torture.

EXECUTION

Although we associate the Tower with imprisonment and executions, only a handful of executions have actually taken place within its walls. At the time, executions within the Tower took place on Tower Green, now a pleasant and unassuming lawn to the west of the White Tower between the Chapel Royal of St Peter ad Vincula and the Queen's House.

The first execution of a prisoner in the Tower is believed to have been William Hastings, Edward IV's former Lord Chancellor, who was imprisoned by the Duke of Gloucester, later Richard III. Richard and Hastings had been boyhood friends, but this didn't stop Richard arresting him on charges of treason – clearly he saw Hastings, who was close to Edward's son, as a threat to his own potential control of the throne.

Axe, Block, and Executioner's Mask.

Incarceration and execution of nobility, even royalty, at the Tower increased sharply during the reigns of the Tudor monarchs. The roll-call of high-status prisoners at the Tower in the 16th and early-17th centuries looks very much like a 'who's who' of the English peerage.

Of Henry VIII's leading advisers, only two – Archbishop Cranmer and Edward Seymour – survived his reign with heads and fortunes intact, such was the fickleness of his regard. Sir Thomas More and Bishop Fisher both died in 1535 for refusing to acknowledge Henry VIII as head of the new Church of England. More was a former Chancellor and a favourite of Henry's, so the king tried many ways to persuade him to recant in the hope of getting the pious churchman to save his life. Thomas Cromwell had his head removed for bungling the marriage to Anne of Cleves and the reconciliation with Europe. Thomas Howard, Duke of Norfolk, survived his relationship to two of Henry's 'adulterous' wives, but was finally condemned to death, along with his son, Henry, when the ageing king began to suspect Howard had his eye on the throne. Henry Howard was beheaded on 19 January 1547 and Thomas only survived because the king pre-deceased him. The 4th Duke, Thomas's grandson, was later executed by Elizabeth I for plotting to marry Mary Queen of Scots and put her on the throne of England.

The first queen to be imprisoned in the Tower was the 'great whore' Anne Boleyn. When her ability to beguile Henry VIII ran out, he accused her of 'following daily her frail and carnal lust' with four men, including her brother. In truth, after forcing the country through a myriad of religious changes to achieve his aim of marrying her, Anne had failed to produce a healthy son and Henry was undoubtedly looking for a scapegoat.

Anne denied the charges against her – incest, plotting to kill the king and sorcery – which were circumstantial to say the least, but she was still found guilty. The men convicted of adultery with her were executed on Tower Hill, but Anne was accorded the privilege of being beheaded in the relative privacy of the Tower. On her arrival at the Tower in 1536, Anne is reported to have asked: 'Shall I go into a dungeon?' and was told: 'No madam, you shall go into the lodging that you lay in at your coronation.' So she watched the preparations for her execution from the windows of the apartment Henry VIII had prepared for her as his bride, just three years earlier.

'Commend me to his Majesty and tell him that he hath ever been constant in his career of advancing me; from a private gentlewoman he hath made me a Marchioness; from a Machioness a Queen, and now that he hath no higher degree of honour he gives my innocency the crown of martyrdom.'

Anne Boleyn's last message to King Henry VIII was deemed so scathing none of his courtiers dared deliver it.

Sentence was carried out in front of the Constable of the Tower on 19 May, just 17 days after she was arrested. When the Master of the Tower told Anne Boleyn her death would not be painful she replied jocularly: 'I heard say the executioner was very good, and I have a little neck.'

She was beheaded in the French style, kneeling up and her head being removed with one slash of a great sword which had been hidden from her view under straw, by an executioner brought from Calais for the occasion.

No one had thought to make any arrangements for the body, and Anne Boleyn's body lay unburied, in an old elm arrow chest as a makeshift coffin, in the Chapel Royal of St Peter ad Vincula. Due to the delay in burial, it was rumoured that the body had been spirited away to be interred at Sale Church, close to Blicking Hall where Anne grew up. Another rumour held that her heart had been removed and was buried within a church in Suffolk. During Queen Victoria's reign the Chapel was renovated and several bodies identified, including those of Henry's two executed queens. Victoria ordered them both reinterred with memorial plaques set in the new marble floor to mark their resting place.

The elderly Countess of Salisbury, Margaret Pole, was executed at the Tower for treason in 1541, but – according to one account – not until she had literally given the executioner a run for his money.

Margaret was daughter of the Duke of Clarence (the one who found his way into the butt of malmsey) and cousin to the Princes in the Tower. On her day of execution, the story goes, the sprightly countess challenged the headsman to do

In Elizabeth's reign, the story of the Greys took on a new twist. Lady Catherine Grey, sister to Lady Jane, took up a position as a rival to the crown out of necessity. As a granddaughter to Henry VIII's younger sister Mary, she had a good claim and her clandestine marriage to the well-connected Edward Seymour, Earl of Hertford, did not help. When Catherine became pregnant and could disguise her pregnancy no longer, the couple were both sent to the Tower in September 1561. Dangerously, Catherine gave birth to a son and then managed to create a scandal when she became pregnant almost immediately afterwards. It transpired that the Lieutenant of the Tower, Edward Warner, had taken pity on the young couple and had allowed them to meet in secret.

his worst and had to be dragged to the block and forced down. After the first clumsy blow she got up and ran. The executioner gave chase, hacking at her head, neck and shoulders 11 times, until he finally subdued her. The sight was, according to witnesses, truly horrific.

Her execution was timed to coincide with Henry VIII's marriage to Catherine Howard, but a short time later Catherine was herself on the scaffold. Around 22 years of age when she died, the vivacious Catherine was Anne Boleyn's first cousin, and had caught Henry's eye while lady-in-waiting to his previous queen, Anne of Cleves. Henry described Catherine as: '[his] very jewel of womanhood', so when rumours of affairs began to circulate less than a year after her marriage he initially ignored them. When, late in 1541, Henry did sanction an investigation, evidence was swiftly gathered to condemn the young queen. On 13 February 1542 she was beheaded in one stroke on Tower Green and, like her cousin, buried in an unmarked grave in the Chapel Royal of St Peter ad Vincula.

One of the most unpopular executions to take place on Tower Green was that of Lady Jane Grey. Lady Jane was great-niece of Henry VIII and declared heir to Henry's only son, the short-lived Edward VI. She was a very scholarly girl with a profound understanding of religion, able to argue the Protestant cause with some of the most learned Catholic theologians, but she had been forced into marriage with Lord Guildford Dudley and

The Earl of Essex was beheaded at Elizabeth I's behest within the precincts of the Tower. He was one of only two men to be executed thus, his **private execution** being ordered because the queen could not risk a public display due to Essex's **popularity**. Among other special preparations, according to contemporary records, **two headsmen** were present so there would be **a spare if the first one fainted.**

is depicted historically as a pawn of her father-in-law, the Duke of Northumberland. On 10 July 1553, four days after Edward's death, Lady Jane Grey became queen, as Northumberland had planned. Almost immediately, Henry VIII's oldest child, Mary, staunch Catholic daughter of his first queen, Catherine of Aragon, raised the support of London and took the throne. Lady Jane was already occupying the royal apartments at the Tower, and changed from monarch to prisoner in just nine days.

While her fate was debated, Lady Jane was held, by tradition, at Number 5 Tower Green, while her husband was imprisoned in the Beauchamp Tower nearby. She was tried on 13 November 1553 at Whitehall and found guilty of high treason, along with her husband. The sentence pronounced that she should be 'burned alive on Tower Hill or beheaded as the Queen pleases'. With her keen moral conscience, Mary sent her own chaplain to try to convert Jane to Catholicism before she met her death. Popular opinion did not favour the execution of such young and unworldly figures as Jane and her teenage husband, and Mary, who had herself been embroiled in intrigue almost from the moment of her birth, seemed to recognise that Lady Jane was an unwilling participant in the political machinations of her elders.

Politics prevailed nevertheless, and the following February the 'nine-day queen' was beheaded, aged just 16. Before her own demise, she watched Lord Guildford being taken from the Tower bound for Tower Hill, and the return of his body, the head wrapped separately in a cloth. Queen Mary had granted them the opportunity to meet on the morning before their executions, but Jane absolutely refused.

OFF WITH HIS HEAD

Henry VIII wasn't the only royal to behead former favourites.
Elizabeth I, the Virgin Queen, sentenced Sir Walter Ralegh to
death in 1618 (see Chapter 6), as well as the youthful Robert
Devereux, 2nd Earl of Essex and son-in-law of Francis
Walsingham, Elizabeth's most enduring adviser. Essex was
openly disdainful of another of her advisers, Sir Robert Cecil,
and often disobeyed royal orders, but his early martial exploits
earned him forgiveness. However, his comeuppance came
during the Nine Years War (1594-1603) when, at his own
insistence, he became Lord Lieutenant of Ireland. With the
largest army ever sent to that country, he still failed to put
down the rebellion and ended up having to negotiate a truce.
Despite the queen's order not to return, in 1599 he boldly
appeared in her bedchamber at Nonsuch Palace while she was
still undressed, relying on her fondness for him, and his
popularity with the ordinary people to see him through. The
Privy Council, however, decided his truce and departure from
Ireland were tantamount to desertion of duty, and he was placed
under house arrest. Recognising he was still a threat, his old
adversary Lord Cecil persuaded Elizabeth to send her former
favourite to trial.

With a retinue of friendly nobles, Essex marched to London,
intending to demand an interview with the monarch. Cecil took
the opportunity to declare it a rebellion and had him arrested
for treason. Essex had a loyal following, and Thomas Lee, a
captain in Essex's Irish army, was found outside the queen's
private chambers, intending to take her hostage until she signed

So many people came to witness the 1747 beheading of 80-year-old Jacobite troublemaker Lord Simon Lovat on Tower Hill, that one of the grandstands erected to allow them a better view collapsed, killing 11 people [although some reports have the death toll as high as 50].

a warrant freeing his former commander – he was tried and executed immediately. And on 19 February 1601 Essex himself was beheaded at the Tower.

The last beheadings to take place on Tower Hill came as a result of the Jacobite Rebellions, aimed at putting the Stuarts back on the throne, at the expense of James II. Among them was the colourful Lord Lovat who had been involved in both rebellions, in 1715 and 1745. Old by the time of the second uprising, the wily lord had told the Jacobites he was with them all the way, although physically too infirm to take much of a role, while telling the government he was loyal and that he regretted his son had gone off without permission to join Bonnie Prince Charlie (in fact, Lovat had to compel his son to go and fight for the rebels).

Following the English victory at Culloden in 1745, Lovat took to the hills; his lands were seized and castles burned. Although he often had to be carried in a litter as he fled, he still had the strength to gather a Jacobite council and plan a counter-attack. Eventually he was tracked down and carried back to London, where he was found guilty of treason. Although reportedly weak, he died cheerfully on 9 April 1747, quoting Horace: '*Dulce et decorum est, pro patria mori* (It is right and fitting to die for one's country).'

AN HONOURABLE EXECUTION

When Carl Hans Lody faced a firing squad on 6 November 1914, he was the first person to be imprisoned then executed at the Tower for more than 150 years. The firing squad was considered an honourable form of execution, done to soldiers, by soldiers. The daring exploits of spies were recognised by this fact, while war criminals, by contrast, were usually hanged.

During World War I, trials were held 'in camera' at the Tower, and after Carl Hans Lody's death, a further 10 men were taken to the Tower charged with spying, and died there, the last on 11 April 1916. The final spy to be executed at the Tower was Sergeant Josef Jakobs in World War II. Jakobs had

Although the majority of the executions took place in the rifle range, two men arrested for spying in 1915, **HPM Janssen and WJ Roos, were shot** in the ditch surrounding the Tower. According to a witness: 'Roos eyed the fatal chair, from which the bleeding body of his accomplice had just been removed, with a **fair show of indifference.'** He smoked a final cigarette and 'with apparently no more interest in the proceedings, he seated himself in the chair. There was a momentary twingeing of the face as they fastened the bandage... he too died bravely, and met his fate **with a courage which could evoke nothing but admiration'.**

been found in a field at night in 1941, having parachuted in with around £500 in pound notes, an attaché case containing a wireless set, a map on which RAF bases were marked, as well as civilian clothing under his flying suit. He was charged with 'committing treachery' and 'intent to help the enemy'.

Jakobs claimed to have flown solo from Luxembourg to join the English war effort, and at his court martial asked to be imprisoned until the end of the war, when he would be able to prove his intentions. But in a communication marked 'Most Secret', the Constable of the Tower was given the following order by Sir Bertram Sergison-Brooke to carry out the last execution at the Tower of London: 'I have the honour to acquaint you that JOSEF JAKOBS, an enemy alien, has been found guilty of an offence against the Treachery Act 1940 and has been sentenced to suffer death by being shot.

'The said enemy alien has been attached to the Holding Battalion, Scots Guards for the purpose of punishment and the execution has been fixed to take place at H.M. Tower of London on Friday the 15th August 1941 at 7.15am.'

The Tower's last execution victim met his fate sitting down because he'd broken his right ankle on landing – the Royal Armouries still has the chair on which he died.

CHAPTER

TRADITIONS OF
THE TOWER

he Tower of London is the most visited historical attraction in the UK, and its long history is enshrined not just in its towers and chambers, but also in the long-held traditions and ceremonies that remain an important and integral part of the Tower's life.

A visit to the Tower of London is linked in most people's minds with the Yeoman Warders, those impressive and genial gentlemen – commonly, but mistakenly, referred to as Beefeaters – in their resplendent uniforms, displaying unfailing good humour and well-versed in every legend, rumour and new development relating to the Tower.

Each day they must deal with thousands of queries from tourists of all nationalities, talk knowledgeably and entertainingly about the Tower and pose for numerous pictures. Before they are permitted to act as public guides, each new Yeoman Warder must learn every detail of the Tower's 900-year history, in order to anticipate the questions of visitors ranging from small children interested in tales of ghosts and murder, to foreign academics fascinated by the niceties of English custom.

Although there are few early records, we know that the Yeoman Warders were established in the 15th century and were originally royal bodyguards; they were an offshoot of the Yeomen of the Guard. Gilbert & Sullivan were not the only ones to confuse them with the Yeomen of the Guard – their operetta 'The Yeomen of the Guard' is actually all about Yeoman Warders. Although they fulfil different roles, the two companies do have a similar uniform, but the full dress uniform of the Yeomen of the Guard is distinguished by a broad scarlet and gold sash over the left shoulder.

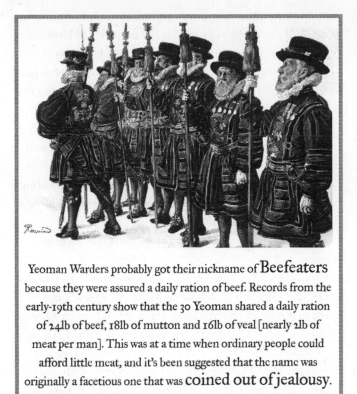

Yeoman Warders probably got their nickname of **Beefeaters** because they were assured a daily ration of beef. Records from the early-19th century show that the 30 Yeoman shared a daily ration of 24lb of beef, 18lb of mutton and 16lb of veal [nearly 2lb of meat per man]. This was at a time when ordinary people could afford little meat, and it's been suggested that the name was originally a facetious one that was **coined out of jealousy**.

As the Tower's use as a royal residence declined, the Yeoman Warders' job description changed, and by the reign of Henry VIII they had became chiefly responsible for guarding prisoners, with whom the Tower was rapidly filling up (see Chapter 6). One Warder was appointed Gentleman Gaoler, and each Warder would be assigned to one or more prisoners. During this period the Warders became known as Waiters, because they waited up on the prisoners in their charge, and were often the only human contact for those in close confinement. To this day, their daily duty roster is called The Wait.

Up until the Civil War, the Yeoman Warders continued to act as part of the Tower's defence force; they were charged with guarding the entrance at all times. Nine men – although not all of them were always Yeoman Warders – guarded it during the day, and six at night. The role of Yeoman Warders as unofficial tour guides increased as prisoner numbers decreased following the upheaval of the Reformation and the Jacobite rebellions. Although early visitors to the Tower came by royal or government invitation, from the middle of the 17th century records show that people were simply turning up with money in their pockets, ready to pay to be shown around.

There are currently just 36 Yeoman Warders (one of whom acts as Raven Master) plus a Chief Yeoman Warder and Yeoman Gaoler, making 38 in total. This is not an enormous number considering that around 2.5 million people visit the Tower annually – that's more than 6,800 a day.

On joining this august band, a new Warder is sworn in at a special ceremony held on Tower Green after the Tower shuts to the public, where they take an oath of allegiance that dates back to 1337, when the Yeoman Warders were still part of the larger King's Bodyguard. After the swearing-in, it's customary for all the Warders to retire indoors and drink punch together.

> **The full title of a Yeoman Warder is:** Yeoman Warder of Her Majesty's Royal Palace and Fortress the Tower of London, and Member of the Sovereign's Body Guard of the Yeoman Guard Extraordinary.

There is symbolic significance even in this convivial tradition. The punch is mixed in a great pewter punch bowl from 1722, which was presented to the Warders by one of their own number who'd been caught moonlighting as an innkeeper in Southwark. The man, named Wilkins, was discovered pulling pints when he should have been carrying pikes at the Tower. Presumably he hoped his generous gesture would help his superiors overlook his dual income.

In 1555, the Constable of the Tower had asked for, and presumably got, 21 'personable Yeomen of middle age' and stipulated they should be over 30 but under 50, seven of whom were made Chief Yeoman Warders. The Constable's records suggest that, in addition to their 8d daily wages (around £6.46 in modern terms), they received tips for showing people around the less accessible parts of the Tower, such as the Armoury or the Mint. But things soon went downhill. The Yeoman Warders' pay failed to keep pace with inflation, which perhaps explains why the Lieutenant of the Tower was complaining that several of them had other jobs on the side in 1598, or had become physically unfit, neglecting their duties, taking instead to drunkenness and brawling.

At this time, it was usual for new Yeoman Warders to inherit or purchase their position, and it is this practice that

> The soldiers you see on ceremonial parade at the Tower can come from **any British or Commonwealth regiment,** although it is traditional for them to be drawn from **Guards regiments.**

is remembered when toasting the new arrival. The Chief Yeoman Warder makes a toast with the words: 'May you never die a Yeoman Warder.' He's not just wishing the new Warder longevity, but referring to the period when the Warder's post was a 'living' that you could purchase for 250 guineas (approximately £35,700 in modern terms) – you paid a lump sum up front as an investment against a regular income for many years. A sum of £250 (approximately £34,000 in modern terms) went to the retiring Warder whose place you were taking, and the 250 extra shillings (approximately £1,712 in modern terms) went to the Constable of the Tower. If you lived to retirement age, your post could be sold and you'd recoup £250 of the original investment; but if you died, the Constable was free to sell the position himself, and pocket the whole 250 guineas, hence the toast.

The Duke of Wellington, who was Constable from 1826 to 1852, changed all that. He decided that, in future, the Yeoman Warders would be upstanding men, non-commissioned officers from the Household Cavalry, Foot Guards or Infantry of the Line, specially recommended by their commanding officers. New payments were introduced for their services as tour guides, and they were no longer allowed to receive gratuities from visitors. In the early days of tourism at the Tower, visitors seem to have been charged according to their grandeur. In some cases, the Yeoman Warders might receive the equivalent of several weeks' wages, if the visitor were important enough (General Patrick Gordon handed out 33s (approximately £165.50 in modern terms) at the various different departments during his visit in 1660), but by the early-18th century, there was enough of a consensus for guide books to give prospective visitors a table of what they would be expected to pay.

Nowadays, Yeoman Warders are all former warrant officers from Her Majesty's Forces with an honourable service record of at least 22 years. They are living links to life at the Tower hundreds of years ago, carrying out ceremonies dating back 700 years or more.

Their distinctive scarlet dress uniform, with its long tunic featuring many embroidered badges, striped braid and starched and ruffled collar, worn with red stockings and black patent leather pumps, has remained essentially unchanged for centuries; the collar gives away its Tudor origins.

Most visitors, however, see them in their blue 'undress' uniform, which was granted to them by Queen Victoria in 1858 as a more practical outfit in which to carry out their duties. The 'undress' uniform is still rather splendid, with its long skirts, decorative embroidery, high splayed hat and frogged cloak, and comes in two different weights for summer and winter wear.

When dressed up for state occasions, the Yeoman Warders also carry an old-fashioned weapon, a kind of pike which is known as a partisan, as well as a ceremonial sword. Back in

Elizabethan times, the Warders had a different sort of pike, which was called a halberd, and during the early-18th century they also carried a brace of pistols. Partisans, although similar, were less effective as a weapon, with a smaller double-headed axe beneath a short spear blade. They soon became obsolete as a combat weapon.

The Yeoman Warders maintain an ancient chain of command just as they maintain their ancient weapons. There is still an official Yeoman Gaoler, second in command to the Chief Yeoman Warder, who can be spotted on state occasions by the axe he carries. These occasions include such infrequent occurrences like the lying in state of dead sovereigns and the coronations of new ones, as well as the annual Lord Mayor's Show.

THE RAVENS

Alongside the Yeoman Warders, the ravens have been symbols of the Tower of London for hundreds of years. The legend goes that if the ravens ever abandon the Tower, the Tower will collapse and the Kingdom will fall.

Charles II reputedly considered getting rid of the ravens, who were getting in the way of the Royal Observatory's attempts to map the stars. Following complaints from John Flamsteed, in charge of the Observatory in the north-eastern turret of the White Tower, the king was ready to banish the ravens until someone recounted the legend to him, at which point he had the Observatory moved, and kept the birds, decreeing that there must always be six ravens at the Tower.

Given his family's track record on the throne, one can hardly blame him; he must have felt he needed all the luck he could get.

Recent research, released in 2004, revealed that a new examination by Tower historians had been unable to find any record of ravens being kept at the Tower before the 19th century. Picturesque legends aside, however, this does not mean for certain that they weren't there before this. No one quite knows when they first started congregating at the Tower, or where the legendary associations with the monarchy originates, but ravens were well known in London during the Medieval period, where they were often seen around the meat markets feasting on leftover scraps.

No one can remember the Tower without its ravens, although during World War II, only one of the ravens survived (a bird called Grip); several are thought to have died of shock during the bombings. The king survived without any apparent harm and the birds' numbers were made up by new stock in time for the Tower's reopening in 1946.

Halberds were extremely useful weapons, consisting of an axe mounted on the top of a long pole, which was finished with a lengthy spike. The pole was often reinforced with metal to catch a sword blade, and the hooked shape of the axe made it effective for grappling and chopping, as well as stabbing at a distance. **A skilled man with a halberd could often bring down an armoured knight.**

The ravens are looked after by one of the Yeoman Warders known as the Raven Master, and one of the current ravens, Thor, has apparently learned to mimic his voice. Among his other daily duties, the Raven Master is responsible for feeding his charges raw meat, whole rabbits and biscuits soaked in blood. However, their favourite treat, which they filch from the mess kitchen leftovers, is apparently fried bread.

Precautions were taken in February 2006 to safeguard the ravens when stories about the spread of avian flu were all over the papers. The birds were removed to the Upper Brick Tower and kept inside in quarantine until 15 May when, on the advice of London Zoo, they were allowed to roam free once more. 'I didn't like having to bring the Tower Ravens inside, but at the time I believed it was the safest thing to do for their own protection, given the speed that the virus was moving across Europe. They seemed to cope well with their confinement and continued to eat well. Thor continued to mimic me, which was a good sign.' reported Raven Master Derrick Coyle.

Ravens were generally considered birds of ill omen in British folklore, and are associated with death. Stories abound of the Tower ravens taking up a position near to a sick person and cawing mournfully, refusing to leave their perch until the person has passed away. But these birds are not universally ill-regarded. In Native North American Indian legend they are tricksters, whose curiosity aids in the creation of the land, and in Norse mythology they were the companions of Odin, his messengers and bringers of wisdom. Their association

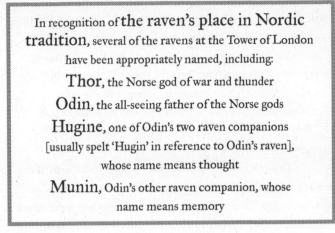

In recognition of **the raven's place in Nordic tradition**, several of the ravens at the Tower of London have been appropriately named, including:

Thor, the Norse god of war and thunder

Odin, the all-seeing father of the Norse gods

Hugine, one of Odin's two raven companions [usually spelt 'Hugin' in reference to Odin's raven], whose name means thought

Munin, Odin's other raven companion, whose name means memory

with kings may have stemmed from their earlier association with gods in Germanic religions.

Seven birds are usually kept in special lodgings beside the Wakefield Tower, so that if one dies unexpectedly the quota can still be met. They all have one wing clipped to prevent them leaving. This method of clipping doesn't stop them flying completely, but it hinders them to such an extent that they're not able to go far. At least that's the theory. One raven called Grog lived up to his name when he disappeared after 21 years at the Tower, and was last sighted outside an East London pub called the Rose and Punchbowl. Ravens can live for a very long time – the longest on record at the Tower being 44 years – so Grog may yet be enjoying a long life on the outside.

The Tower established its own raven-breeding programme in 1987, although Odin and Thor, the second youngest birds currently at the Tower, were both rescued as fledglings by the Owl Sanctuary in the New Forest, and arrived to join the Tower's group in 1997. The newest arrival is Baldrick, named after *Blackadder*'s comic buffoon with a cunning plan rather than a Norse god.

A RESIDENCE AND A MONUMENT

It's easy to regard the Tower solely as a historic monument, and not realise that it is also home to many families with members employed in the roles necessary to keep it functioning, including the Resident Governor and all the Yeoman Warders. In total, about 150 people can be found within the Tower when it's locked up for the night.

The Governor traditionally occupies the Queen's House, while the Warders are given grace and favour houses – some are ancient rooms within the thickness of the Tower's outer wall. Warders must also maintain another residence outside of the Tower, however, so that they do not become homeless when they retire.

In addition to the 'live-in' staff, about 100 non-residents work there every day. Not only are they there to run an important tourist attraction, and maintain the building's historic fabric, but they are also there to take part in the ceremonial life of the Tower, which is as important today as it has been for centuries.

The Ceremony of the Keys, which takes place just before 10pm every night, is believed to be the oldest surviving continuous military ceremony in the world. Its exact origin is somewhat obscure, but some historians believe it dates back to the early days of the White Tower, when the citizens of London didn't always see eye to eye with their Norman overlords, and there was a great need for tight security. Originally, the Chief Yeoman Warder and his guard would probably go around checking and locking all of the Tower of London's gates and doors.

It was the Duke of Wellington who moved the ceremony to the current time of 10pm, to allow his soldiers plenty of time to return to their barracks following an evening enjoying themselves in the city, without getting locked out – although thanks to some soldiers' memoirs we know they had ways of breaking into the Tower by shinning up drainpipes and going over the roofs, should they miss the curfew.

The Ceremony (which members of the public may apply to attend), is run like clockwork. The Chief Yeoman Warder comes out of the Byward Tower carrying a traditional candle lantern in one hand and the Queen's Keys in the other. The lantern was presented to the Yeoman Warders on 12 May 1919 by members of the 1st Reserve Battalion of the Honourable Artillery Company as a memento of the happy times they had spent garrisoned at the Tower.

The Chief Yeoman Warder walks to the Bloody Tower to collect his escort – a sergeant and a drummer – who march with him to the Middle Tower and then the Byward Tower, stopping to lock the great oak doors of both. They then proceed along Water Lane towards the Wakefield Tower, but when they pass the Bloody Tower they are stopped with the word: 'Halt'. They are then challenged by a sentry who asks: 'Who comes there?' In a ritual exchange, the Chief Yeoman

> '...there shall be a place appointed under Locke and key where in the keys of the gates of the saide Tower shall be laide in the sight of the constable, the porter and **two of the Yeoman Warders**, or three of them at the least... And the key of that locke or coffer where the keys be, to be kepte by the porter or, in his absence, by the **chiefe yeoman warder**.'
>
> *Instructions dating from 1555 to ensure the security of the Tower of London. It is still used in the Ceremony of the Keys*

Warder replies: 'The Keys.' He is then asked: 'Who's Keys?' He replies: 'Queen Elizabeth's Keys.'

After passing the sentry, the party receives the salute from the Guard for the night, and the Chief Yeoman Warder waves his hat in the air and shouts: 'God preserve Queen Elizabeth.' All of this takes precisely seven minutes, timed so that the parade ground clock chimes 10pm as the cheer dies down, and the drummer, who has accompanied the Chief Yeoman Warder, sounds 'Last Post' on his bugle (you might expect a bugler to be more suitable for the task, but tradition demands a drummer, so a drummer they have). Finally, the Queen's Keys are ceremoniously taken to the house of the Resident Governor for safekeeping overnight.

Other colourful ceremonies open to the public are the State Parades, which take place within the Tower's walls on the mornings of Easter Sunday, Whitsun and the Sunday before Christmas. The Yeoman Warders, in their full regalia, accompany the Governor from the Queen's House to the Chapel Royal of St Peter ad Vincula for a special service.

Any visitor can watch the parade, but to go into the service you must have permission which, like that for attending the Ceremony of the Keys, is obtained in writing beforehand.

A much more private ceremony, known as the Ceremony of the Roses and the Lilies, is held every year on 21 May, at around 6.30pm. It commemorates the death of King Henry VI on that day in 1471, supposedly struck down in the Oratory in the Wakefield Tower some time between 11pm and midnight. Although Henry may have died as a result of despair and illness brought on by the death of his son and the arrest of his wife, rumour abounded that this religious, if irresolute, former monarch was murdered at prayer by Edward IV (see Chapter 6). Whatever the truth, this gentle king is remembered every year by the two educational establishments he founded.

Today the Oratory, which is set in a recess off the main chamber, contains an altar chest – a kind of portable altar – which shows the arms of King's College Cambridge and Eton College, both founded by Henry VI. In 1923, an old Etonian, Thomas Buchanan Carter, with the help of Sir George Youngblood, then Keeper of the Jewel House, arranged to have a marble tablet set in the Oratory on the spot where Henry was supposed to have fallen, and ever since Eton lilies have been laid there as a mark of remembrance. Even during World War II, when the Wakefield Tower was hit by a German bomb, the ceremony continued. To ensure the longevity of the ceremony, Carter's two sons, John and Will had a book privately printed by the Rampant Lion Press, which detailed the correct procedure.

In 1947 King's College Cambridge was granted permission by George VI to join the ceremony, and began laying a bunch of white roses, tied with a regal purple ribbon, alongside the pale [not blue!] lilies. At the ceremony each year, the Provost or Deputy Provost of the two educational institutions and the Chaplain of the Tower are conducted by the Resident Governor from the Queen's House to the Wakefield Tower, accompanied by a guard of Yeoman Warders. After a short service, the Provosts lay their flowers, which remain in the Oratory until dusk the next day.

An irregular ceremony is that of the Constable's Dues, commemorating the time when the Constable was entitled to a cut of almost everything that passed the Tower on the river. A large Royal Navy vessel moors alongside the Tower and an escort of Yeoman Warders in scarlet state dress along with a corps of drums set out to meet it. They escort the captain of the vessel and his own escort of naval ratings back to the Tower, carrying a barrel of rum to be ceremonially presented to the governor of the Tower. A more recent (and no doubt very welcome) tradition is for all participants to retire to the Queen's House to sample the contents of the barrel after the ceremony is completed!

Every three years, on Ascension Day, local children and Tower officials go around the perimeter of the area known as the Tower Liberties – a small area around the castle precinct which is under the jurisdiction of the Tower itself, rather than the surrounding City of London – and hit the boundary stones with willow wands. This ceremony, known as Beating the Bounds, harks back to the 14th century practice of

Constable's Dues

By royal decree, the Constable of the Tower is entitled
to a number of perks, including:

A barrel of wine from every ship carrying
wine up the Thames

Any swans swimming between London Bridge and
the sea [presumably for the dinner table]

Any horses, cows, pigs, sheep or oxen
that fall off London Bridge into the river

Nowadays, he has to make do with a ceremonial
barrel of rum delivered by the Royal Navy.

beating local boys at or over the boundary stones – now the boys get their revenge, it seems.

One of the least frequent Tower ceremonies is the installation of a new Constable of the Tower. The post becomes vacant every five years, and the new Constable is officially welcomed by the Lord Chamberlain, representing her Majesty, on Tower Green, where he hands over the gold keys to the Tower. The new Constable then gives the keys of the Queen's House to the Resident Governor, granting him permission to live there: his first official duty.

Along with Hyde Park, the Tower is one of London's traditional stations for gun salutes. Salutes are fired each year to celebrate a number of royal anniversaries and other special occasions, and the Honourable Artillery Company is in charge of firing salutes from the Tower of London's guns, which are aimed out over the Thames.

Although it has become an **honorary post**, in the early days, the **Constable of the Tower of London** was responsible for:

Maintaining the buildings

Paying the garrison

Ensuring the security of prisoners

Supervising the numerous departments housed at the Tower, such as the **Royal Menagerie, Wardrobe** and **Records Office**

Ensuring the security of the Crown Jewels and other valuables

Keeping order in the City of London

And, **until 1290**, regulating and protecting the Jewish community in London

Perhaps unsurprisingly, the Tower's salute is different from others around the country. The standard salute is 21 rounds, and 41 for a royal palace and fortress (the State Opening of Parliament and visiting heads of state receive 41). But in 1828, a further 21 guns were added for all royal occasions as a special mark of respect from the City of London, making the Tower salute 62 in all.

Extremely rarely, an 124-gun salute is fired on 10 June, when the Queen's official birthday coincides with the Duke of Edinburgh's actual birthday. The last time this happened was in 1967, which means that, fittingly, the Tower probably holds the record for the most rounds ever fired in a single salute to its sovereign.

BIBLIOGRAPHY

✠

Albion: A Guide to Legendary Britain, Jennifer Westwood
A New History of the Royal Mint, CE Challis
The Beefeaters of the Tower of London, G Abbott
The Cecils of Hatfield House, David Cecil
Church and State, Clair Cross
The Crown Jewels Official Guidebook, Anna Keay
Death Comes to the Maiden: Sex and Execution 1431-1933,
Camille Nais
The Elizabethan Renaissance (2 vols), AL Rowse
Henry VIII: King & Court, Alison Weir
The Lancaster and York: Wars of the Roses, Alison Weir
The Last Plantagenets, Thomas B Costain
The Lives of the Kings and Queens of England, Antonia Fraser
Mysteries of the Tower of London, G Abbott
New Oxford History of England, Julian Hoppit
Oxford History of England Vol 3, AL Poole
Oxford History of England Vol 4, Sir Maurice Powicke
Oxford History of England Vol 5, May McKisack
Prisoners of the Tower, Jeremy Ashbee
Richard III, Charles Ross
The Six Wives of Henry VIII, Antonia Fraser
Torture: Tower of London, David Birt
The Tower Menagerie, Daniel Hahn
The Tower of London: The Official Illustrated History, Edward
Impey & Geoffrey Parnell
Travesties and Transgressions in Tudor and Stuart England,
David Cressy

HISTORIC
ROYAL PALACES

Historic Royal Palaces is an independent charity that
looks after the Tower of London, Hampton Court Palace,
the Banqueting House, Kensington Palace State
Apartments and Kew Palace.

Our aim is to help everyone explore the story of
how monarchs and people have shaped society, in
some of the greatest palaces ever built.

Each of the five royal palaces in our care has survived for
hundreds of years. They have witnessed peace and
prosperity and splendid periods of building and
expansion, but they also share stories of more turbulent
times, of war and domestic strife, politics and revolution.

Although the palaces are owned by The Queen
on behalf of the nation, we receive no funding from
the government or the Crown, so we depend on
the support of our visitors, donors, sponsors,
members and volunteers.